TABLE OF CONTENT

Arabic Grammar (Nahw)

The Four
Characteristics
of Nouns

ISM—The Arabic Noun

الْإِسْم

♦ The ISM—Arabic Noun is that KALIMAH(Word) which is independent of other words in conveying its meaning and devoid of any of the three tenses

♦ The ISM—Arabic noun includes the following:

- Name of a person
  * Hamid, Maryam, Khalid, Umar
- Name of a place
  * Egypt, Arabia, School, Store
- Thing
  * Book, Pen, Camera, Table
- Adjective
  * Tall, Short, Boring, Exciting
- Adverb
  * Slowly, Happily, Quickly, Gently
- Idea (Verbal Noun—verb not confined to a specific time period)
  * Justice, Happiness, Education, Authority

♦ When we mention the name of "ALLAH" linguistically, we avoid saying "the word ALLAH" or "the name ALLAH" in order to give proper respect to ALLAH SWT and to prevent using His name in a casual way. Instead, we say Lafz ul Ja-laalah [ ], the Grand Word.

♦ Nouns have four important characteristics. These are (DING):

Definite—Indefinite		Gender— جِنْس		I'rab— إِعْرَاب		Number— عَدَد	
Definite	مَعْرِفَةٌ	Masculine	مُذَكَّر	Rafa'	رَفْع	Singular	وَاحِد
Indefinite	نَكِرَةٌ	Feminine	مُؤَنَّث	Nasb	نَصْب	Dual	تَثْنِيَة
				Jarr	جَرّ	Plural	جَمْع

Definite and Indefinite

1. Definite or Specific (مَعْرِفَةٌ)

- A definite noun refers to a specific thing.

- Zaid (زَيْدٌ) is the name of a particular person.

- Makkah (مَكَّةٌ) is the name of a specific city

- The man (اَلرَّجُلُ) – refers to a specific person

2. Indefinite or Common (نَكِرَةٌ)

- An indefinite noun is a word which refers to a general thing.

- The word – (رَجُلٌ) a man, does not refer to any specific person. It can refer to any person

- The word – (طَيِّبٌ) does not refer to any particular good thing. Every good thing can be called (طَيِّبٌ)

- There are no definite or indefinite articles in Arabic language equivalent to English a, an, the

- Since اِسْمٌ cannot at the same time be definite and indefinite, تَنْوِيْن and اَلْ do not coexist

  اَلْقَلَمٌ and اَلْكِتَابٌ will be incorrect

- تَنْوِيْن is also used with proper nouns i.e. خَالِدٌ .. زَيْدٌ .. مُحَمَّدٌ Even though there is a تَنْوِيْن at the end of the noun, these proper nouns are definite

Definite and Indefinite

Drill #1

Look at each word and identify the type (common or proper) of the word:

	Word	Type	Reason		Word	Type	Reason
1	شَيْءٍ	Indefinite / Common	Tanween at the end	18	هُوْدٌ		
2	كَنَدَا	Definite/Proper	Name of place	19	مَطَرٌ		
3	مَرْيَمُ			20	الْفَاكِهَةَ		
4	أَمْرِيْكَ			21	مُحَمَّدًا		
5	يَا صَالِحُ			22	يَا وَلَدُ!		
6	كِتَابٍ			23	رَجُلٌ		
7	الْحِبْرُ			24	شَجَرَةً		
8	لِبَاسًا			25	السَّبُّوْرَةِ		
9	السَّمَآءَ			26	مِرْسَمًا		
10	الْأُسْتَاذَ			27	نُوْحًا		
11	مِحْبَرًا			28	كَبِيْرًا		
12	مُصْلِحَةٌ			29	مَكْتَبَةً		
13	شَمْسٍ			30	الْقُرْءَانِ		
14	النَّجْمَةِ			31	حَقِيْبَةٌ		
15	أَرْضٍ			32	الْمَدْرَسَةِ		
16	مِبْرَاةً			33	يَوْمٍ		
17	الْكُرَّاسَةُ			34	الزَّهْرَةَ		

Definite and Indefinite

Drill #2

Identify Type(Common/Proper) of the under line words in the following Aayah fragments

TYPE (2)	TYPE (1)	Ayah	
		فِى قُلُوبِهِم مَّرَضٌ فَزَادَهُمُ اللَّهُ مَرَضًا 2:10	1
		أُولَٰئِكَ الَّذِينَ اشْتَرَوُا الضَّلَالَةَ بِالْهُدَىٰ 2:16	2
		وَاللَّهُ مُحِيطٌ بِالْكَافِرِينَ 2:19	3
		بَلَاءٌ مِّن رَّبِّكُمْ عَظِيمٌ 14:6	4
		إِنَّ اللَّهَ عَلَىٰ كُلِّ شَىْءٍ قَدِيرٌ 2:20	5
		الَّذِى جَعَلَ لَكُمُ الْأَرْضَ فِرَاشًا 2:22	6
		وَأَنزَلَ مِنَ السَّمَاءِ مَاءً 2:22	7
		فَأَخْرَجَ بِهِ مِنَ الثَّمَرَاتِ رِزْقًا لَّكُمْ 2:22	8
		وَقُودُهَا النَّاسُ وَالْحِجَارَةُ ۖ أُعِدَّتْ لِلْكَافِرِينَ 2:23	9
		ثُمَّ اسْتَوَىٰ إِلَى السَّمَاءِ فَسَوَّاهُنَّ سَبْعَ سَمَاوَاتٍ 2:29	10
		وَإِذْ قَالَ رَبُّكَ لِلْمَلَائِكَةِ إِنِّى جَاعِلٌ فِى الْأَرْضِ خَلِيفَةً 2:30	11
		وَإِذْ قُلْنَا لِلْمَلَائِكَةِ اسْجُدُوا لِآدَمَ فَسَجَدُوا إِلَّا إِبْلِيسَ 2:34	12
		وَقُلْنَا يَا آدَمُ اسْكُنْ أَنتَ وَزَوْجُكَ الْجَنَّةَ وَكُلَا مِنْهَا رَغَدًا حَيْثُ شِئْتُمَا 2:35	13
		وَلَكُمْ فِى الْأَرْضِ مُسْتَقَرٌّ وَمَتَاعٌ إِلَىٰ حِينٍ 2:36	14
		وَأَقِيمُوا الصَّلَاةَ وَآتُوا الزَّكَاةَ وَارْكَعُوا مَعَ الرَّاكِعِينَ 2:43	15
		وَاسْتَعِينُوا بِالصَّبْرِ وَالصَّلَاةِ ۚ وَإِنَّهَا لَكَبِيرَةٌ إِلَّا عَلَى الْخَاشِعِينَ 2:45	16
		وَإِذْ نَجَّيْنَاكُم مِّنْ آلِ فِرْعَوْنَ يَسُومُونَكُمْ سُوءَ الْعَذَابِ 2:49	17
		وَإِذْ وَاعَدْنَا مُوسَىٰ أَرْبَعِينَ لَيْلَةً 2:51	18
		ثُمَّ اتَّخَذْتُمُ الْعِجْلَ مِن بَعْدِهِ وَأَنتُمْ ظَالِمُونَ 2:51	19
		وَقُولُوا حِطَّةٌ نَّغْفِرْ لَكُمْ خَطَايَاكُمْ ۚ وَسَنَزِيدُ الْمُحْسِنِينَ 2:58	20

Definite and Indefinite

Drill #3

Convert definite to indefinite or indefinite to definite

	Word	Conjugate		Word	Conjugate		Word	Conjugate
1	شَيْءٍ		18	الْبَيْتُ		35	شَمْعَةٌ	
2	الْجَنَّةَ		19	مَطَرٌ		36	الرَّأْسَ	
3	سَحَابٌ		20	الْفَاكِهَةَ		37	فِرَاشًا	
4	نَهَارًا		21	مِصْبَاحٌ		38	مِلْعَقَةً	
5	الْجَمِيلِ		22	الطَّاوِلَةِ		39	الْكُرْسِيُّ	
6	كِتَابٍ		23	رَجُلٌ		40	السَّاعَةِ	
7	الْحِبْرُ		24	شَجَرَةً		41	غُرْفَةٍ	
8	لِبَاسًا		25	السَّبُّوْرَةِ		42	صَحْنٍ	
9	السَّمَآءَ		26	مِرْسَمًا		43	الْقِدْرَ	
10	الْأُسْتَاذَ		27	الْمِفْتَاحُ		44	سِكِّيْنٍ	
11	مِحْبَرًا		28	كَبِيْرًا		45	طَوِيْلٌ	
12	مُصْلِحَةٌ		29	مَكْتَبَةٌ		46	الصَّابُوْنَ	
13	شَمْسٍ		30	الْبُسْتَانَ		47	قُفْلًا	
14	النَّجْمَةِ		31	حَقِيْبَةٌ		48	مَكْتَبٌ	
15	أَرْضٍ		32	الْمَدْرَسَةِ		49	سُلَّمٌ	
16	مِبْرَاةً		33	يَوْمٍ		50	ثَلَّاجَةٌ	
17	الْكُرَّاسَةُ		34	الزَّهْرَةُ		51	الْوِسَادَةُ	

Vocabulary Crosswords

CLASS ROOM

English to Arabic:

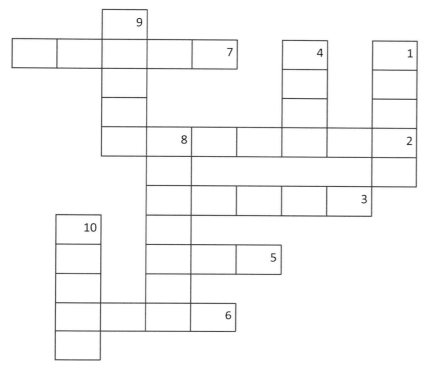

DOWN	**ACROSS**
1. pens	2. school
4. pencil	3. bags
8. black-boards	5. ink
9. notebook	6. book
10. inkpots	7. sharpener

Arabic to English:

DOWN	**ACROSS**
2 مِحْبَرٌ	1 كُتُبٌ
5 قَلَمٌ	3 كُرَّاسَاتٌ
7 حَقِيْبَةٌ	4 مَرَاسِمُ
8 سَبُّوْرَةٌ	6 أَسَاتِذَة
9 مِمْحَاةٌ	
10 مَدَارِس	

Gender

Signs of Feminine Nouns

Most of the words ending with "Taa Marbutaah" ة at the end

Ruler	مِسْطَرَةٌ	Car	سَيَّارَةٌ	Window	نَافِذَةٌ	Skillful (F)	مَاهِرَةٌ
Teacher (F)	مُعَلِّمَةٌ	Room	غُرْفَةٌ	Beautiful (F)	جَمِيْلَةٌ	Table	طَاوِلَةٌ

Word ending with a ى but pronounced like Alif (ا) also called "Alif Maqsurah"

صُغْرَىٰ	أَفْعَىٰ	لَيْلَىٰ	كُبْرَىٰ	عُظْمَىٰ

Word ending with a اء long Alif Hamza also called "Alif Mamdudah"

صَفْرَاءُ	سَوْدَاءُ	بَيْضَاءُ	خَضْرَاءُ	زَرْقَاءُ	صَحْرَاءُ	سَمَاءٌ

Body parts in pairs

Leg	رِجْلٌ	Hand	يَدٌ	Ear	أُذُنٌ	Eye	عَيْنٌ
Shoulder	كَعْبٌ	Elbow	مِرْفَقٌ	Foot	قَدَمٌ	Arm	ذِرَاعٌ

Biological Feminine (Feminine by their linguistic meaning)

Bride	عُرُوْسٌ	Sister	أُخْتٌ	Daughter	بِنْتٌ	Mother	أُمٌّ

Whatever the Arabs defined as feminine

Knife	سِكِّيْنٌ	Wind	رِيْحٌ	Fire	نَارٌ	Sun	شَمْسٌ
Person	نَفْسٌ	Ship	فُلْكٌ	House	دَارٌ	War	حَرْبٌ
Wine	خَمْرٌ	Hell	جَهَنَّمُ	Land	أَرْضٌ	Path	سَبِيْلٌ
Cup	كَأْسٌ	Well	بَئْرٌ	Staff	عَصَا	Bucket	دَلْوٌ

Gender

Drill #4

Look at each word and identify the gender of the word:

	Word	Gender	Reason		Word	Gender	Reason
1	لَيْلَى			18	كُبْرَى		
2	كَنَدَا			19	مَطَرٌ		
3	مَرْيَمُ			20	الْفَاكِهَةَ		
4	أَمْرِيْكَ			21	أُمٌّ		
5	حَمْرَاءُ			22	الْعُيُوْنِ		
6	كِتَابٍ			23	رَجُلٌ		
7	الْحِبْرُ			24	شَجَرَةً		
8	لِبَاسًا			25	السَّبُّوْرَةِ		
9	السَّمَآءَ			26	مِرْسَمًا		
10	الْأُسْتَاذَةُ			27	رِجْلٌ		
11	مِحْبَرًا			28	نُوْحًا		
12	مُصْلِحَةٌ			29	مَكْتَبَةً		
13	شَمْسٍ			30	الْقُرْءَانِ		
14	النَّجْمَةِ			31	حَقِيْبَةٌ		
15	أَرْضٍ			32	الْمَدْرَسَةِ		
16	مِبْرَاةً			33	يَوْمٍ		
17	الْكُرَّاسَةُ			34	الزَّهْرَةَ		

Gender

Drill #5

Identify the GENDER of the under line words in the following Aayah fragments

Gender (2)	Gender (1)	Ayah	
		نَارُ اللَّهِ الْمُوقَدَةُ 104:6	1
		تَرْمِيهِم بِحِجَارَةٍ مِّن سِجِّيلٍ 105:4	2
		إِنَّ الْإِنسَانَ لِرَبِّهِ لَكَنُودٌ 100:6	3
		رَسُولٌ مِّنَ اللَّهِ يَتْلُو صُحُفًا مُّطَهَّرَةً 98:2	4
		وَجَعَلْنَا فِيهَا جَنَّاتٍ مِّن نَّخِيلٍ وَأَعْنَابٍ وَفَجَّرْنَا فِيهَا مِنَ الْعُيُونِ 36:34	5
		وَاذْكُرْ فِي الْكِتَابِ مَرْيَمَ إِذِ انتَبَذَتْ مِنْ أَهْلِهَا مَكَانًا شَرْقِيًّا 19:16	6
		وَأَنزَلَ مِنَ السَّمَاءِ مَاءً 2:22	7
		وَهُوَ الَّذِي خَلَقَ اللَّيْلَ وَالنَّهَارَ وَالشَّمْسَ وَالْقَمَرَ ۖ كُلٌّ فِي فَلَكٍ يَسْبَحُونَ 21:33	8
		كُلُّ نَفْسٍ ذَائِقَةُ الْمَوْتِ 21:35	9
		وَتَاللَّهِ لَأَكِيدَنَّ أَصْنَامَكُم بَعْدَ أَن تُوَلُّوا مُدْبِرِينَ 21:57	10
		وَإِذْ قَالَ رَبُّكَ لِلْمَلَائِكَةِ إِنِّي جَاعِلٌ فِي الْأَرْضِ خَلِيفَةً 2:30	11
		وَإِذْ قُلْنَا لِلْمَلَائِكَةِ اسْجُدُوا لِآدَمَ فَسَجَدُوا إِلَّا إِبْلِيسَ 2:34	12
		وَقُلْنَا يَا آدَمُ اسْكُنْ أَنتَ وَزَوْجُكَ الْجَنَّةَ وَكُلَا مِنْهَا رَغَدًا حَيْثُ شِئْتُمَا 2:35	13
		وَلَكُمْ فِي الْأَرْضِ مُسْتَقَرٌّ وَمَتَاعٌ إِلَىٰ حِينٍ 2:36	14
		وَأَقِيمُوا الصَّلَاةَ وَآتُوا الزَّكَاةَ وَارْكَعُوا مَعَ الرَّاكِعِينَ 2:43	15
		وَاسْتَعِينُوا بِالصَّبْرِ وَالصَّلَاةِ ۚ وَإِنَّهَا لَكَبِيرَةٌ إِلَّا عَلَى الْخَاشِعِينَ 2:45	16
		وَإِذْ نَجَّيْنَاكُم مِّنْ آلِ فِرْعَوْنَ يَسُومُونَكُمْ سُوءَ الْعَذَابِ 2:49	17
		وَإِذْ وَاعَدْنَا مُوسَىٰ أَرْبَعِينَ لَيْلَةً 2:51	18
		ثُمَّ اتَّخَذْتُمُ الْعِجْلَ مِن بَعْدِهِ وَأَنتُمْ ظَالِمُونَ 2:51	19
		وَقُولُوا حِطَّةٌ نَّغْفِرْ لَكُمْ خَطَايَاكُمْ ۚ وَسَنَزِيدُ الْمُحْسِنِينَ 2:58	20

Gender

Drill #6

Convert masculine to feminine or feminine to masculine

	Word	Conjugate		Word	Conjugate		Word	Conjugate
1	الْمُعَلِّمُ		18	عَالِمٌ		35	الطَّبَّاخَةَ	
2	مُهَنْدِسَةٍ		19	مَعْلُوْمَةٌ		36	عَمٌّ	
3	خَالٌ		20	قَوِيٌّ		37	لَاعِبٍ	
4	الطَّالِبَةِ		21	شَاكِرَةٌ		38	تِلْمِيْذَةٌ	
5	اِبْنَةً		22	مَلِكٌ		39	مَفْتُوْحًا	
6	الْجَمِيْلِ		23	الْقَادِرَ		40	سَهْلٌ	
7	قَبِيْحَةً		24	عَزِيْزَةٌ		41	صَعْبَةٍ	
8	الْمُغْلَقَةُ		25	شَرِيْفَةٌ		42	نَظِيْفًا	
9	صَغِيْرًا		26	مَقْتُوْلًا		43	وَسِخَةٌ	
10	الْأُسْتَاذَ		27	النَّاصِرَةُ		44	الْجَدِيْدُ	
11	كَاذِبَةً		28	كَبِيْرًا		45	طَوِيْلٌ	
12	مُصْلِحَةٌ		29	الْجَدَّةُ		46	الْقَدِيْمَةِ	
13	حَفِيْدًا		30	الْبَخِيْلَ		47	كَرِيْمًا	
14	السَّرِيْعَةَ		31	سَعِيْدَةٌ		48	حَزِيْنٌ	
15	بَطِئٌ		32	ذَكِيًّا		49	الْغَنِيُّ	
16	جَيِّدَةً		33	الرَّدِئُ		50	جَالِسَةٍ	
17	الذَّاكِرُ		34	خَالِصَةً		51	زَاهِدًا	

Grammatical States

Arabic Name	Case / Sign	Function in a sentence	Example
مَرْفُوْعٌ	Dammah (ُ) two Dammahs (ٌ)	Subject Doer of a verb	الْكِتَابُ ثَقِيْلٌ ضَرَبَ زَيْدٌ حَامِدًا
مَنْصُوْبٌ	Fathah (َ) two Fathahs (ً)	Object of a verb	نَصَرَ رَجُلٌ وَلَدًا نَصَرَ وَلَدًا رَجُلٌ
مَجْرُوْرٌ	Kasrah (ِ) two Kasrahs (ٍ)	Possessor of a thing, or comes after a preposition or an adverb	بَيْتُ الرَّجُلِ فِي مَسْجِدٍ تَحْتَ الْمَكْتَبِ

- When a word is ending with two Fathahs, Alif is need to be added to the end of the word.

  E.g. مُحَمَّدًا / كِتَابًا / رَسُوْلًا

- There are two exceptions to the above rule:

  The words ending with Taa Marbutaah

  E.g. جَنَّةً / أَيَةً / نَافِذَةً

  The words ending with Alif and Hamza

  E.g. سَمَاءً / بَيْضَاءً

Grammatical States

Drill #7

Look at the end of each word and identify the status of the word:

	Word	Status		Word	Status		Word	Status
1	شَيْءٍ		18	الْبَيْتُ		35	شَمْعَةٌ	
2	الْجَنَّةَ		19	مَطَرٌ		36	الرَّأْسَ	
3	سَحَابٌ		20	الْفَاكِهَةَ		37	فِرَاشًا	
4	نَهَارًا		21	مِصْبَاحٌ		38	مِلْعَقَةً	
5	الْجَمِيلِ		22	الطَّاوِلَةِ		39	الْكُرْسِيُّ	
6	كِتَابٍ		23	رَجُلٌ		40	السَّاعَةِ	
7	الْحِبْرُ		24	شَجَرَةً		41	غُرْفَةٍ	
8	لِبَاسًا		25	السَّبُّوْرَةِ		42	صَحْنٍ	
9	السَّمَآءَ		26	مِرْسَمًا		43	الْقِدْرَ	
10	الْأُسْتَاذَ		27	الْمِفْتَاحُ		44	سِكِّيْنٍ	
11	مِحْبَرًا		28	كَبِيْرًا		45	طَوِيْلٌ	
12	مُصْلِحَةٌ		29	مَكْتَبَةٌ		46	الصَّابُوْنَ	
13	شَمْسٍ		30	الْبُسْتَانَ		47	قُفْلًا	
14	النَّجْمَةِ		31	حَقِيْبَةٌ		48	مَكْتَبٌ	
15	أَرْضٍ		32	الْمَدْرَسَةِ		49	سُلَّمٌ	
16	مِبْرَاةً		33	يَوْمٍ		50	ثَلَّاجَةٌ	
17	الْكُرَّاسَةُ		34	الزَّهْرَةَ		51	الْوِسَادَةُ	

Grammatical States

Drill #8

Identify the STATE of the under line words in the following Aayah fragments

STATE (2)	STATE (1)	Ayah	
		نَارُ اللَّهِ الْمُوقَدَةُ 104:6	1
		تَرْمِيهِم بِحِجَارَةٍ مِّن سِجِّيلٍ 105:4	2
		إِنَّ الْإِنسَانَ لِرَبِّهِ لَكَنُودٌ 100:6	3
		رَسُولٌ مِّنَ اللَّهِ يَتْلُو صُحُفًا مُّطَهَّرَةً 98:2	4
		وَجَعَلْنَا فِيهَا جَنَّاتٍ مِّن نَّخِيلٍ وَأَعْنَابٍ وَفَجَّرْنَا فِيهَا مِنَ الْعُيُونِ 36:34	5
		وَاذْكُرْ فِي الْكِتَابِ مَرْيَمَ إِذِ انتَبَذَتْ مِنْ أَهْلِهَا مَكَانًا شَرْقِيًّا 19:16	6
		وَأَنزَلَ مِنَ السَّمَاءِ مَاءً 2:22	7
		وَهُوَ الَّذِي خَلَقَ اللَّيْلَ وَالنَّهَارَ وَالشَّمْسَ وَالْقَمَرَ ۖ كُلٌّ فِي فَلَكٍ يَسْبَحُونَ 21:33	8
		كُلُّ نَفْسٍ ذَائِقَةُ الْمَوْتِ 21:35	9
		وَتَاللَّهِ لَأَكِيدَنَّ أَصْنَامَكُم بَعْدَ أَن تُوَلُّوا مُدْبِرِينَ 21:57	10
		وَإِذْ قَالَ رَبُّكَ لِلْمَلَائِكَةِ إِنِّي جَاعِلٌ فِي الْأَرْضِ خَلِيفَةً 2:30	11
		وَإِذْ قُلْنَا لِلْمَلَائِكَةِ اسْجُدُوا لِآدَمَ فَسَجَدُوا إِلَّا إِبْلِيسَ 2:34	12
		وَقُلْنَا يَا آدَمُ اسْكُنْ أَنتَ وَزَوْجُكَ الْجَنَّةَ وَكُلَا مِنْهَا رَغَدًا حَيْثُ شِئْتُمَا 2:35	13
		وَلَكُمْ فِي الْأَرْضِ مُسْتَقَرٌّ وَمَتَاعٌ إِلَى حِينٍ 2:36	14
		وَأَقِيمُوا الصَّلَاةَ وَآتُوا الزَّكَاةَ وَارْكَعُوا مَعَ الرَّاكِعِينَ 2:43	15
		وَاسْتَعِينُوا بِالصَّبْرِ وَالصَّلَاةِ ۚ وَإِنَّهَا لَكَبِيرَةٌ إِلَّا عَلَى الْخَاشِعِينَ 2:45	16
		وَإِذْ نَجَّيْنَاكُم مِّنْ آلِ فِرْعَوْنَ يَسُومُونَكُمْ سُوءَ الْعَذَابِ 2:49	17
		قَالَ رَبِّ اجْعَل لِّي آيَةً ۚ قَالَ آيَتُكَ أَلَّا تُكَلِّمَ النَّاسَ ثَلَاثَ لَيَالٍ سَوِيًّا 19:10	18
		إِنَّ الَّذِينَ آمَنُوا وَعَمِلُوا الصَّالِحَاتِ كَانَتْ لَهُمْ جَنَّاتُ الْفِرْدَوْسِ نُزُلًا 18:107	19
		قَالَ إِنَّمَا أَنَا رَسُولُ رَبِّكِ لِأَهَبَ لَكِ غُلَامًا زَكِيًّا 19:19	20

Grammatical States

Drill #9

Write the State (R/N/J), Gender (M/F) and Type (C/P) above the underline words

C/M/J

وَإِن كُنتُمْ عَلَىٰ سَفَرٍ وَلَمْ تَجِدُوا كَاتِبًا فَرِهَانٌ مَّقْبُوضَةٌ ۖ فَإِنْ أَمِنَ بَعْضُكُم بَعْضًا

فَلْيُؤَدِّ الَّذِي اؤْتُمِنَ أَمَانَتَهُ وَلْيَتَّقِ اللَّهَ رَبَّهُ ۗ وَلَا تَكْتُمُوا الشَّهَادَةَ ۚ وَمَن يَكْتُمْهَا

فَإِنَّهُ آثِمٌ قَلْبُهُ ۗ وَاللَّهُ بِمَا تَعْمَلُونَ عَلِيمٌ ۝ لِّلَّهِ مَا فِي السَّمَاوَاتِ وَمَا فِي

الْأَرْضِ ۗ وَإِن تُبْدُوا مَا فِي أَنفُسِكُمْ أَوْ تُخْفُوهُ يُحَاسِبْكُم بِهِ اللَّهُ ۖ فَيَغْفِرُ لِمَن

يَشَاءُ وَيُعَذِّبُ مَن يَشَاءُ ۗ وَاللَّهُ عَلَىٰ كُلِّ شَيْءٍ قَدِيرٌ ۝ آمَنَ الرَّسُولُ بِمَا أُنزِلَ إِلَيْهِ

مِن رَّبِّهِ وَالْمُؤْمِنُونَ ۚ كُلٌّ آمَنَ بِاللَّهِ وَمَلَائِكَتِهِ وَكُتُبِهِ وَرُسُلِهِ لَا نُفَرِّقُ بَيْنَ أَحَدٍ مِّن

رُّسُلِهِ ۚ وَقَالُوا سَمِعْنَا وَأَطَعْنَا ۖ غُفْرَانَكَ رَبَّنَا وَإِلَيْكَ الْمَصِيرُ ۝ لَا يُكَلِّفُ اللَّهُ

نَفْسًا إِلَّا وُسْعَهَا ۚ لَهَا مَا كَسَبَتْ وَعَلَيْهَا مَا اكْتَسَبَتْ ۗ رَبَّنَا لَا تُؤَاخِذْنَا إِن نَّسِينَا

أَوْ أَخْطَأْنَا ۚ رَبَّنَا وَلَا تَحْمِلْ عَلَيْنَا إِصْرًا كَمَا حَمَلْتَهُ عَلَى الَّذِينَ مِن قَبْلِنَا ۚ رَبَّنَا وَلَا

تُحَمِّلْنَا مَا لَا طَاقَةَ لَنَا بِهِ ۖ وَاعْفُ عَنَّا وَاغْفِرْ لَنَا وَارْحَمْنَا ۚ أَنتَ مَوْلَانَا فَانصُرْنَا

عَلَى الْقَوْمِ الْكَافِرِينَ ۝

Miftaah Institute — Education | Preservation | Application — 17

Vocabulary Crosswords

NATURE

English to Arabic:

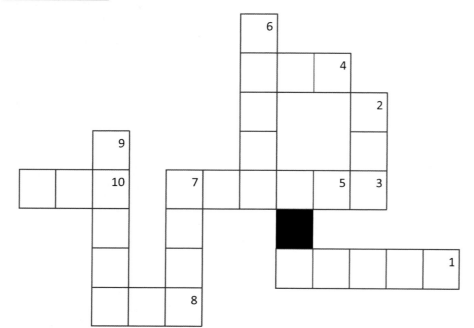

DOWN	ACROSS
2. grass	1. dry fruits
5. cloud	3. gardens
6. leaves	4. moon
7. stars	8. rain
9. trees	10. sun

Arabic to English:

DOWN	ACROSS
1. سُحُبٌ	2. وَرَقَةٌ
4. بُسْتَانٌ	3. أَزْهَارٌ
9. فَاكِهَةٌ	5. نَهَارٌ
10. سَمَاوَاتٌ	6. لَيْلَةٌ
	7. نَجْمَةٌ
	8. أَغْصَانٌ

Number

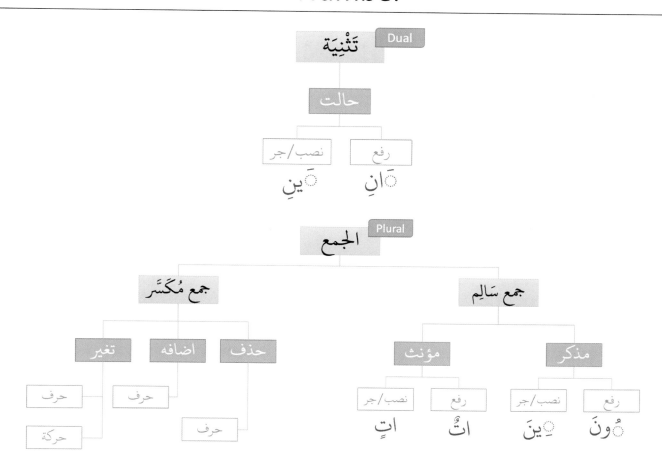

	Broken Plurals					
	المعنى	جمع	مفرد	المعنى	جمع	مفرد
	one of a pair	أَزْوَاجٌ	زَوْجٌ	witness	شُهَدَاءُ	شَاهِدٌ
	emotional heart	أَفْئِدَةٌ	فُؤَادٌ	blessing	نِعَمٌ	نِعْمَةٌ
	woman	نِسَاءٌ	اِمْرَأَةٌ	prophet	أَنْبِيَاءُ	نَبِيٌّ

Plural by meaning			
	المعنى	الكلمة	المعنى	الكلمة
	an argumentative group	خَصْمٌ	a nation	قَوْمٌ
	a faction	حِزْبٌ	a people	نَاسٌ
	an army	جُنْدٌ	a generation	قَرْنٌ
	family / people	آلٌ	family / people	أَهْلٌ

Grammatical States/Number/Masculine Charts

Drill #10

Plural جَمْعٌ	Dual مُثَنَّى	Singular مُفْرَدٌ	
صَالِحُوْنَ	صَالِحَانِ	صَالِحٌ	Rafa'
صَالِحِيْنَ	صَالِحَيْنِ	صَالِحًا	Nasb
صَالِحِيْنَ	صَالِحَيْنِ	صَالِحٍ	Jarr

Plural جَمْعٌ	Dual مُثَنَّى	Singular مُفْرَدٌ	
		مُسْلِمٌ	Rafa'
			Nasb
			Jarr

Plural جَمْعٌ	Dual مُثَنَّى	Singular مُفْرَدٌ	
		مُوْمِنٌ	Rafa'
			Nasb
			Jarr

When you have learnt the Muslim chart please find 3 different people in your class to sign off your charts and after that read it to the instructor/TA for final sign off

Masculine Noun Chart—Memorization Tracker				
Noun	Person 1	Person 2	Person 3	Instructor/TA
مُسْلِمٌ				

Education | Preservation | Application

Grammatical States/Number/Feminine Charts

Drill #11

Plural جَمْعٌ	Dual مُثَنَّى	Singular مُفْرَدٌ	
صَالِحَاتٌ	صَالِحَتَانِ	صَالِحَةٌ	Rafa'
صَالِحَاتٍ	صَالِحَتَيْنِ	صَالِحَةً	Nasb
صَالِحَاتٍ	صَالِحَتَيْنِ	صَالِحَةٍ	Jarr

Plural جَمْعٌ	Dual مُثَنَّى	Singular مُفْرَدٌ	
		مُسْلِمَةٌ	Rafa'
			Nasb
			Jarr

Plural جَمْعٌ	Dual مُثَنَّى	Singular مُفْرَدٌ	
		مُوْمِنَةٌ	Rafa'
			Nasb
			Jarr

When you have learnt the Muslimah chart please find 3 different people in your class to sign off your charts and after that read it to the instructor/TA for final sign off

Feminine Noun Chart—Memorization Tracker				
Noun	Person 1	Person 2	Person 3	Instructor/TA
مُسْلِمَةٌ				

Number

Drill #12

Write singular/dual/plural for each word given:

	Word	Number		Word	Number		Word	Number
1	الْمُعَلِّمُ		18	الظُّلُمَاتِ		35	الطَّبَّاخَتَانِ	
2	مُهَنْدِسُوْنَ		19	مَعْلُوْمَتَيْنِ		36	قَانِتُوْنَ	
3	شَاهِدَانِ		20	مُفْسِدَتَانِ		37	لَاعِبَانِ	
4	الطَّالِبَةِ		21	خَالِدِيْنَ		38	تِلْمِيْذَاتٍ	
5	صَالِحَاتٍ		22	مَلِكٌ		39	مُحَمَّدًا	
6	الْجَمِيْلَانِ		23	آيَاتٌ		40	مُؤْمِنُوْنَ	
7	قَبِيْحَتَيْنِ		24	مَاكِثِيْنَ		41	مُؤْمِنِيْنَ	
8	الْقُرْءَانِ		25	سَمَاوَاتٍ		42	نَظِيْفَيْنِ	
9	مُؤْمِنَانِ		26	مَقْتُوْلَيْنِ		43	وَسِخَةٌ	
10	الْأُسْتَاذَ		27	النَّاصِرَاتِ		44	كُتُبٌ	
11	كَاذِبَاتٌ		28	كَبِيْرَانِ		45	طَوِيْلَانِ	
12	حَقِيْبَةٌ		29	الْجَدَّتَانِ		46	الْمِرْسَمُ	
13	حَفِيْدُوْنَ		30	الْبَخِيْلُوْنَ		47	كَرِيْمَاتٍ	
14	قَلَمَيْنِ		31	سَعِيْدِيْنَ		48	الصَّابُوْنَ	
15	الْبُسْتَانَ		32	ذَكِيَّانِ		49	شَجَرَةً	
16	الْمَدْرَسَةِ		33	مَكْتَبٌ		50	جَالِسَاتٌ	
17	الذَّاكِرُوْنَ		34	خَالِصَاتٍ		51	زَاهِدِيْنَ	

Number

Drill #13

Write singular/dual/plural for each underlined word in the Aayah fragments below:

Number (2)	Number (1)	Ayah	
		وَمِن شَرِّ النَّفَّاثَاتِ فِي الْعُقَدِ 113:4	1
		وَمَا أُمِرُوا إِلَّا لِيَعْبُدُوا اللَّهَ مُخْلِصِينَ لَهُ الدِّينَ حُنَفَاءَ 98:5	2
		إِلَّا الَّذِينَ آمَنُوا وَعَمِلُوا الصَّالِحَاتِ فَلَهُمْ أَجْرٌ غَيْرُ مَمْنُونٍ 95:6	3
		وَيَقُولُونَ مَتَىٰ هَٰذَا الْوَعْدُ إِن كُنتُمْ صَادِقِينَ 36:48	4
		وَجَعَلْنَا فِيهَا جَنَّاتٍ مِّن نَّخِيلٍ وَأَعْنَابٍ وَفَجَّرْنَا فِيهَا مِنَ الْعُيُونِ 36:34	5
		هَٰذَا مَا وَعَدَ الرَّحْمَٰنُ وَصَدَقَ الْمُرْسَلُونَ 36:52	6
		إِنَّ أَصْحَابَ الْجَنَّةِ الْيَوْمَ فِي شُغُلٍ فَاكِهُونَ 36:55	7
		رَبُّ الْمَشْرِقَيْنِ وَرَبُّ الْمَغْرِبَيْنِ 55:17	8
		وَأَمَّا إِن كَانَ مِنَ الْمُكَذِّبِينَ الضَّالِّينَ 56:92	9
		فِيهِمَا عَيْنَانِ نَضَّاخَتَانِ 55:66	10
		وَإِذْ قَالَ رَبُّكَ لِلْمَلَائِكَةِ إِنِّي جَاعِلٌ فِي الْأَرْضِ خَلِيفَةً 2:30	11
		كَانَتَا تَحْتَ عَبْدَيْنِ مِنْ عِبَادِنَا صَالِحَيْنِ فَخَانَتَاهُمَا 66:10	12
		وَصَدَّقَتْ بِكَلِمَاتِ رَبِّهَا وَكُتُبِهِ وَكَانَتْ مِنَ الْقَانِتِينَ 66:12	13
		وَالْوَالِدَاتُ يُرْضِعْنَ أَوْلَادَهُنَّ حَوْلَيْنِ كَامِلَيْنِ ۖ لِمَنْ أَرَادَ أَن يُتِمَّ الرَّضَاعَةَ 2:233	14
		وَأَقِيمُوا الصَّلَاةَ وَآتُوا الزَّكَاةَ وَارْكَعُوا مَعَ الرَّاكِعِينَ 2:43	15
		أَلَمْ نَجْعَل لَّهُ عَيْنَيْنِ ۝ وَلِسَانًا وَشَفَتَيْنِ ۝ 90:8/9	16
		الْخَبِيثَاتُ لِلْخَبِيثِينَ وَالْخَبِيثُونَ لِلْخَبِيثَاتِ 24:26	17
		وَالذَّاكِرِينَ اللَّهَ كَثِيرًا وَالذَّاكِرَاتِ أَعَدَّ اللَّهُ لَهُم مَّغْفِرَةً وَأَجْرًا عَظِيمًا 33:35	18
		تَبَارَكَ الَّذِي نَزَّلَ الْفُرْقَانَ عَلَىٰ عَبْدِهِ لِيَكُونَ لِلْعَالَمِينَ نَذِيرًا 25:1	19
		وَقَالُوا مَالِ هَٰذَا الرَّسُولِ يَأْكُلُ الطَّعَامَ وَيَمْشِي فِي الْأَسْوَاقِ 25:7	20

Number

Drill #14

Look at each word and identify the gender of the word:

	Singular	Dual	Plural		Singular	Dual	Plural
1		قَلَمَانِ		18			كُتُبٌ
2	مِرْسَمًا			19	رِجْلٌ		
3	شَجَرَةٍ			20	الْفَاكِهَةَ		
4	مِحْبَرًا			21	أُمٌّ		
5	السَّبُّورَةِ			22			الْعُيُوْنِ
6		صَالِحَانِ		23		رَجُلَانِ	
7			وَرَقَاتٌ	24	حَقِيْبَةٌ		
8	الزَّهْرَةَ			25	بُسْتَانٌ		
9			أَبْوَابٌ	26			ثَمَرَاتٌ
10		الْأُسْتَاذَتَانِ		27	شَمْسٍ		
11		بَيْتَانِ		28	الْمَدْرَسَةِ		
12			جُدُرًا	29		شَاكِرَانِ	
13		مِلْعَقَتَانِ		30			مَفَاتِيْحَ
14	وِسَادَةً			31	طَاوِلَةٌ		
15		أَبَانِ		32		مَكْتَبَانِ	
16			كَرَاسِي	33	صَحْنٌ		
17	أُخْتٍ			34		مُسْلِمَتَانِ	

Review

Drill #15

Look at the end of each word and identify the status, number, gender and type for each word:

	Word	Status	Number	Gender	Type
1	اَلثَّلَّاجَتَانِ				
2	مُسْلِمَتَيْنِ				
3	العُيُونُ				
4	مُظْلِمُوْنَ				
5	اَقْلَامًا				
6	الْمَلَكَيْنِ				
7	قَائِمَاتٍ				
8	الظَّالِمِيْنَ				
9	صَالِحَتَانِ				
10	الْكُتُبِ				
11	عَيْنَانِ				
12	مَاكِثِيْنَ				
13	مُؤْمِنَانِ				
14	الْحَوَارِيُّوْنَ				
15	سَمَاوَاتٍ				
16	الْمُقَرَّبِيْنَ				
17	الْغَيْبُ				
18	مُدْهَآمَّتَانِ				

Drill #16

Write all the four properties of Ism for the underlined words

الْحَمْدُ لِلَّهِ الَّذِى أَنزَلَ عَلَىٰ عَبْدِهِ الْكِتَابَ وَلَمْ يَجْعَل لَّهُ عِوَجًا ۜ ١ قَيِّمًا لِّيُنذِرَ بَأْسًا

شَدِيدًا مِّن لَّدُنْهُ وَيُبَشِّرَ الْمُؤْمِنِينَ الَّذِينَ يَعْمَلُونَ الصَّالِحَاتِ أَنَّ لَهُمْ أَجْرًا حَسَنًا ٢ مَّاكِثِينَ فِيهِ

أَبَدًا ٣ وَيُنذِرَ الَّذِينَ قَالُوا اتَّخَذَ اللَّهُ وَلَدًا ٤ مَّا لَهُم بِهِ مِنْ عِلْمٍ وَلَا لِآبَائِهِمْ ۚ كَبُرَتْ كَلِمَةً تَخْرُجُ

مِنْ أَفْوَاهِهِمْ ۚ إِن يَقُولُونَ إِلَّا كَذِبًا ٥ فَلَعَلَّكَ بَاخِعٌ نَّفْسَكَ عَلَىٰ آثَارِهِمْ إِن لَّمْ يُؤْمِنُوا بِهَٰذَا الْحَدِيثِ

أَسَفًا ٦ إِنَّا جَعَلْنَا مَا عَلَى الْأَرْضِ زِينَةً لَّهَا لِنَبْلُوَهُمْ أَيُّهُمْ أَحْسَنُ عَمَلًا ٧ وَإِنَّا لَجَاعِلُونَ مَا عَلَيْهَا

صَعِيدًا جُرُزًا ٨ أَمْ حَسِبْتَ أَنَّ أَصْحَابَ الْكَهْفِ وَالرَّقِيمِ كَانُوا مِنْ آيَاتِنَا عَجَبًا ٩ إِذْ أَوَى الْفِتْيَةُ

إِلَى الْكَهْفِ فَقَالُوا رَبَّنَا آتِنَا مِن لَّدُنكَ رَحْمَةً وَهَيِّئْ لَنَا مِنْ أَمْرِنَا رَشَدًا ١٠ فَضَرَبْنَا عَلَىٰ آذَانِهِمْ فِي

الْكَهْفِ سِنِينَ عَدَدًا ١١ ثُمَّ بَعَثْنَاهُمْ لِنَعْلَمَ أَيُّ الْحِزْبَيْنِ أَحْصَىٰ لِمَا لَبِثُوا أَمَدًا ١٢ نَّحْنُ نَقُصُّ عَلَيْكَ

نَبَأَهُم بِالْحَقِّ ۚ إِنَّهُمْ فِتْيَةٌ آمَنُوا بِرَبِّهِمْ وَزِدْنَاهُمْ هُدًى ١٣ وَرَبَطْنَا عَلَىٰ قُلُوبِهِمْ إِذْ قَامُوا فَقَالُوا رَبُّنَا رَبُّ

السَّمَاوَاتِ وَالْأَرْضِ لَن نَّدْعُوَ مِن دُونِهِ إِلَٰهًا ۖ لَّقَدْ قُلْنَا إِذًا شَطَطًا ١٤ هَٰؤُلَاءِ قَوْمُنَا اتَّخَذُوا مِن دُونِهِ

آلِهَةً ۖ لَّوْلَا يَأْتُونَ عَلَيْهِم بِسُلْطَانٍ بَيِّنٍ ۖ فَمَنْ أَظْلَمُ مِمَّنِ افْتَرَىٰ عَلَى اللَّهِ كَذِبًا ١٥

Vocabulary Crosswords

HOUSE HOLD

English to Arabic:

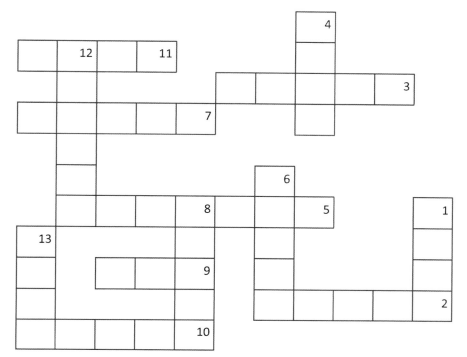

DOWN	ACROSS
1. cups	2. curtain
4. wall	3. sinks
6. spoon	5. refrigera-tors
8. hair combs	7. lamp
12. pillows	9. forks
13. candle	10. table
	11. pots

Arabic to English:

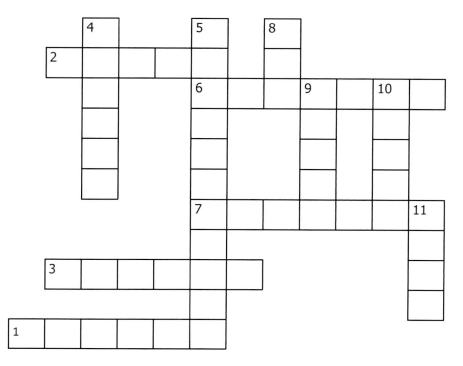

DOWN	ACROSS
4. سَاعَاتٌ	1. كَرَاسِيُّ
5. تِلْفَازَاتٌ	2. صَحْنٌ
8. فِرَاشٌ	3. شُبَّاكٌ
9. مَكَاتِبُ	6 . سَلَالِمُ
10. مِذْيَاعٌ	7. مِقَصٌّ
11. سَجَّادٌ	

Huroof Jarr

Huroof Jarr

Drill #17

مِنْ	وَ	لِ	كَ	تَ	بِ
from	oath	for/have	like	swear	With
	إِلَى	حَتَّى	عَلَى	عَنْ	فِيْ
	towards/to	until	upon/against	about/away	in

When you have learnt the Huroof Jarr chart please find 3 different people in your class to sign off your charts and after that read it to the instructor/TA for final sign off

Huroof Jarr Chart—Memorization Tracker				
Particle	Person 1	Person 2	Person 3	Instructor/TA
Huroof Jarr				

Correct the Jaar Wa Majroor fragments:

	Fragment	Corrected		Fragment	Corrected
1	عَلَى سَيَّارَاتٌ		13	مِنَ الْمُؤْمِنَانِ	
2	إِلَى الْمَدْرَسَةَ		14	وَالزَّيْتُوْنُ	
3	تَاللهَ		15	فِيْ الْفَاكِهَةَ	
4	لِصَادِقُوْنَ		16	وَالشَّمْسِ	
5	كَنَافِدَاتٌ		17	مِنَ الْعُيُوْنَ	
6	بِكِتَابَ		18	كَرَجُلٌ	
7	مِنَ الْحِبْرُ		19	لِشَجَرَةً	
8	بِلِبَاسًا		20	عَلَى السَّبُّوْرَةُ	
9	مِنَ السَّمَآءَ		21	كَمِرْسَمَانِ	
10	إِلَى الْأُسْتَاذَةُ		22	حَتَّىْ حِيْنٌ	
11	كَمِحْبَرًا		23	عَنْ نُوْحًا	
12	لِمُصْلِحُوْنَ		24	مِنَ الشَّاكِرُوْنَ	

Huroof Jarr

Drill #18

Huroof Jarr					
مِنْ	وَ	ل	كَ	تَ	بِ
from	oath	for/have	like	swear	With
	إِلَى	حَتَّى	عَلَى	عَنْ	فِيْ
	towards/to	until	upon/against	about/away	in

School	الْمَدْرَسَةُ	The father	الأَبُّ
Chair	كُرْسِيٌّ	pen	قَلَمٌ
Phone	حَاتِفٌ	Sister	أُخْتٌ
Boy	وَلَدٌ	Masjid	مَسْجِدٌ
Girl	بِنْتٌ	Morning	صُبْحٌ

Translate the following phrases:

	English	Arabic
1	On the chair	
2	In the school	
3	Like a girl	
4	From a phone	
5	(swear) By Allah	
6	To the Masjid	
7	Until morning	
8	(swear) By the pen	
9	About the father	
10	With a boy	
11	For the sister	
12	Upon the schools	
13	From the masjids(2)	

Huroof Jarr

Drill #19

Find the Harf Jarr and Majroor

Majroor	Harf Jarr	Ayah	
		الَّذِينَ يُؤْمِنُونَ بِالْغَيْبِ 2:3	1
		وَبِالْآخِرَةِ هُمْ يُوقِنُونَ 2:4	2
		وَمِنَ النَّاسِ مَن يَقُولُ آمَنَّا 2:8	3
		وَمَا هُم بِمُؤْمِنِينَ 2:8	4
		إِنَّكَ عَلَى الْحَقِّ الْمُبِينِ 27:79	5
		وَيَا قَوْمِ مَا لِي أَدْعُوكُمْ إِلَى النَّجَاةِ وَتَدْعُونَنِي إِلَى النَّارِ 40:41	6
		فَتَوَلَّ عَنْهُمْ حَتَّىٰ حِينٍ 37:174	7
		قَالُوا تَاللَّهِ إِنَّكَ لَفِي ضَلَالِكَ الْقَدِيمِ 12:95	8
		وَأَمَّا إِن كَانَ مِنَ الْمُكَذِّبِينَ الضَّالِّينَ 56:92	9
		سَلَامٌ هِيَ حَتَّىٰ مَطْلَعِ الْفَجْرِ 97:5	10
		وَإِذْ قَالَ رَبُّكَ لِلْمَلَائِكَةِ إِنِّي جَاعِلٌ فِي الْأَرْضِ خَلِيفَةً 2:30	11
		وَاللَّيْلِ إِذَا يَسْرِ 89:4	12
		وَصَدَّقَتْ بِكَلِمَاتِ رَبِّهَا وَكُتُبِهِ وَكَانَتْ مِنَ الْقَانِتِينَ 66:12	13
		فَجَعَلَهُمْ كَعَصْفٍ مَأْكُولٍ 105:5	14
		إِنَّ اللَّهَ لَا يَخْفَىٰ عَلَيْهِ شَيْءٌ فِي الْأَرْضِ وَلَا فِي السَّمَاءِ 3:5	15
		أَلَمْ تَرَ كَيْفَ ضَرَبَ اللَّهُ مَثَلًا كَلِمَةً طَيِّبَةً كَشَجَرَةٍ طَيِّبَةٍ أَصْلُهَا ثَابِتٌ 14:24	16
		الْخَبِيثَاتُ لِلْخَبِيثِينَ وَالْخَبِيثُونَ لِلْخَبِيثَاتِ 24:26	17
		الَّذِينَ هُمْ عَن صَلَاتِهِمْ سَاهُونَ 107:5	18
		تَبَارَكَ الَّذِي نَزَّلَ الْفُرْقَانَ عَلَىٰ عَبْدِهِ لِيَكُونَ لِلْعَالَمِينَ نَذِيرًا 25:1	19
		وَقَالُوا مَالِ هَٰذَا الرَّسُولِ يَأْكُلُ الطَّعَامَ وَيَمْشِي فِي الْأَسْوَاقِ 25:7	20

Mawsoof
Siffah

Mawsoof Siffah

- It's a compound NOT a complete sentence

- Noun comes first and adjective follows

- A single noun can have ONE to MORE adjectives

- Noun and adjective must match on all FOUR properties

صِفَةٌ	مَوْصُوْفٌ
الْمُجْتَهِدَةُ	الطَّالِبَةُ
مَعْرِفَةٌ	مَعْرِفَةٌ
مُؤَنَّثٌ	مُؤَنَّثٌ
مَرْفُوْعٌ	مَرْفُوْعٌ
وَاحِدٌ	وَاحِدٌ

English	Arabic	English	Arabic
The heavy book	الْكِتَابُ الثَّقِيْلُ	A beautiful girl	بِنْتٌ جَمِيْلَةٌ
A big house	بَيْتٌ كَبِيْرٌ	The engineer Zaid	زَيْدٌ الْمُهَنْدِسُ
The clean board	السَّبُّوْرَةُ النَّظِيْفَةُ	The broken pens	اَلْاَقْلَامُ الْمَكْسُوْرَةُ

Mawsoof Siffah

Drill #20

Identify correct Mawsoof Siffah, if not correct them:

	Fragment	Corrected		Fragment	Corrected
1	مَكَانٍ بَعِيْدٍ		17	الطَّالِبَاتُ الشَّاكِرَاتُ	
2	السَّاعَةُ قَرِيْبٌ		18	الرَّجُلَانِ صَالِحَانِ	
3	شَىْءٍ قَدِيْرًا		19	طِفْلٍ صَغِيْرٍ	
4	الْمَسْجِدِ الْحَرَامِ		20	الزَّوْجَةُ صَالِحَةٌ	
5	الْأَرْضَ كِفَاتًا		21	الصُّنْدُوْقِ الْقَدِيْمِ	
6	الْأَرْضَ الْمُقَدَّسَةَ		22	خَادِمَةٌ أَمِيْنًا	
7	رَسُوْلٍ كَرِيْمٍ		23	مُهَنْدِسُوْنَ كَرِيْمُوْنَ	
8	رِيْحٍ طَيِّبَةً		24	الْمُنَافِقِيْنَ كَثِيْرُوْنَ	
9	شَىْءٌ عَجِيْبٌ		25	وَرْدَتَيْنِ جَمِيْلَتَيْنِ	
10	الشَّيْطَانِ الرَّجِيْمِ		26	بَقَرَةٌ صَفْرَاءُ	
11	سَقْفٌ مُرْتَفِعٌ		27	صَالِحَةٌ تَقِيَّةً	
12	نَفْسٍ وَاحِدَةٌ		28	بَابَانِ مَفْتُوْحٌ	
13	سِحْرٌ مُبِيْنٌ		29	الرِّجَالُ الْكَرِيْمُ	
14	الدَّارَ الْآخِرَةَ		30	الْوَلَدَيْنِ صَغِيْرَيْنِ	
15	كَلِمَةً طَيِّبَةً		31	الْحَدِيْقَةِ الْوَاسِعَةِ	
16	لُغَةٌ سَهْلٌ		32	الْبُسْتَانُ جَمِيْلٍ	

Mawsoof Siffah

Drill #21

Underline the Mawsoof Siffah fragments

	Ayah
1	وَقُلْنَا مَا نَزَّلَ اللَّهُ مِن شَيْءٍ إِنْ أَنتُمْ إِلَّا فِي ضَلَالٍ كَبِيرٍ 67:9
2	إِنَّ الَّذِينَ يَخْشَوْنَ رَبَّهُم بِالْغَيْبِ لَهُم مَّغْفِرَةٌ وَأَجْرٌ كَبِيرٌ 67:12
3	أَفَمَن يَمْشِي مُكِبًّا عَلَىٰ وَجْهِهِ أَهْدَىٰ أَمَّن يَمْشِي سَوِيًّا عَلَىٰ صِرَاطٍ مُّسْتَقِيمٍ 67:22
4	قُلْ إِنَّمَا الْعِلْمُ عِندَ اللَّهِ وَإِنَّمَا أَنَا نَذِيرٌ مُّبِينٌ 67:26
5	إِنَّكَ عَلَى الْحَقِّ الْمُبِينِ 27:79
6	قُلْ أَرَأَيْتُمْ إِنْ أَهْلَكَنِيَ اللَّهُ وَمَن مَّعِيَ أَوْ رَحِمَنَا فَمَن يُجِيرُ الْكَافِرِينَ مِنْ عَذَابٍ أَلِيمٍ 67:28
7	قُلْ أَرَأَيْتُمْ إِنْ أَصْبَحَ مَاؤُكُمْ غَوْرًا فَمَن يَأْتِيكُم بِمَاءٍ مَّعِينٍ 67:30
8	وَإِنَّكَ لَعَلَىٰ خُلُقٍ عَظِيمٍ 68:4
9	وَأَمَّا إِن كَانَ مِنَ الْمُكَذِّبِينَ الضَّالِّينَ 56:92
10	فَعَصَوْا رَسُولَ رَبِّهِمْ فَأَخَذَهُمْ أَخْذَةً رَّابِيَةً 69:10
11	كُلُوا وَاشْرَبُوا هَنِيئًا بِمَا أَسْلَفْتُمْ فِي الْأَيَّامِ الْخَالِيَةِ 69:24
12	إِنَّهُ كَانَ لَا يُؤْمِنُ بِاللَّهِ الْعَظِيمِ 69:33
13	وَهَٰذَا لِسَانٌ عَرَبِيٌّ مُّبِينٌ 16:103
14	فَجَعَلَهُمْ كَعَصْفٍ مَّأْكُولٍ 105:5
15	وَقَالَ الْمَلِكُ إِنِّي أَرَىٰ سَبْعَ بَقَرَاتٍ سِمَانٍ يَأْكُلُهُنَّ سَبْعٌ عِجَافٌ وَسَبْعَ سُنبُلَاتٍ خُضْرٍ وَأُخَرَ يَابِسَاتٍ 12:43
16	أَلَمْ تَرَ كَيْفَ ضَرَبَ اللَّهُ مَثَلًا كَلِمَةً طَيِّبَةً كَشَجَرَةٍ طَيِّبَةٍ أَصْلُهَا ثَابِتٌ 14:24
17	فِيهَا عَيْنٌ جَارِيَةٌ ۝ فِيهَا سُرُرٌ مَّرْفُوعَةٌ ۝ وَأَكْوَابٌ مَّوْضُوعَةٌ ۝ 88:12/13/14
18	اهْدِنَا الصِّرَاطَ الْمُسْتَقِيمَ 1:5
19	وَقَالَ رَجُلٌ مُّؤْمِنٌ مِّنْ آلِ فِرْعَوْنَ يَكْتُمُ إِيمَانَهُ أَتَقْتُلُونَ رَجُلًا 40:28
20	هُوَ الَّذِي يُرِيكُمُ الْبَرْقَ خَوْفًا وَطَمَعًا وَيُنشِئُ السَّحَابَ الثِّقَالَ 13:12

Mawsoof Siffah

Drill #22

Tall/long	طَوِيْلٌ	Cold	بَارِدٌ	Window	نَافِذَةٌ	Student	طَالِبٌ
Fast	سَرِيعٌ	Water	مَاءٌ	Ugly	قَبِيْحٌ	hardworking	مُجْتَهِدٌ
Horse	حِصَانٌ	Lesson	دَرْسٌ	Man	رَجُلٌ	Active	نَشِيْطٌ
Brother	أَخٌ	Pen	قَلَمٌ	Street	شَارِعٌ	Smart	ذَكِيٌّ
Easy	سَهْلٌ	Open	مَفْتُوْحٌ	Old	قَدِيْمٌ	Skillful	مَاهِرٌ
Cook	طَبَّاخٌ	House	بَيْتٌ	Big	كَبِيْرٌ	Beautiful	جَمِيْلٌ

Translate the following phrases into Arabic

	English	Arabic		English	Arabic
1.	The tall, horse		4.	The cold water	
2.	The tall brothers(2)		5.	A beautiful, long	
3.	An easy Lesson		6.	An open window	

Translate the following phrases into English

	Arabic	English		Arabic	English
1.	رَجُلٌ قَبِيْحٌ		4.	طَالِبَانِ ذَكِيَّانِ	
2.	الشَّارِعُ الطَّوِيْلُ الْقَدِيْمُ		5.	الطَّبَّاخَةُ الْمَاهِرَةُ	
3.	طَالِبَةٌ مُجْتَهِدَةٌ نَشِيْطَةٌ		6.	بَيْتٌ كَبِيْرٌ جَمِيْلٌ	

Mawsoof Siffah

Drill #23

Form 5 Mawsoof Siffah fragments using the words in the word bank. Conjugate the sentences in both male and female form.

Tall	طَوِيْلٌ		Car	سَيَّارَةٌ	
Beautiful	جَمِيْلٌ		Scholar (F)	عَالِمَةٌ	
Generous	كَرِيْمٌ		Child	طِفْلٌ	
Student	طَالِبٌ		Kind	لَطِيْفٌ	

	English	Arabic
1		
2		
3		
4		
5		
6		
7		
8		
9		
10		
11		
12		
13		

Mawsoof Siffah

Drill #24

Fill empty spots with appropriate mawsoof siffah fragment:

	Singular	Dual	Plural
1	صَالِحَةٌ تَقِيَّةٌ		
2	صَالِحَةً تَقِيَّةً		
3	صَالِحَةٍ تَقِيَّةٍ		
4		الرَّجُلَانِ صَالِحَانِ	
5			أُمَّهَاتٌ صَابِرَاتٌ
6		مُهَنْدِسَيْنِ جَدِيدَيْنِ	
7	الزَّوْجَةُ الصَّالِحَةُ		
8			الْمُنَافِقِيْنَ الْكَاذِبِيْنَ
9		مُعَلِّمَانِ ذَكِيَّانِ	
10			الطَّالِبُوْنَ الصَّالِحُوْنَ
11	طِفْلٍ صَغِيْرٍ		
12		طَبَّاخَتَيْنِ نَظِيْفَتَيْنِ	
13			الرِّجَالُ الْكَرِيْمُوْنَ
14		الْوَلَدَيْنِ الصَّغِيْرَيْنِ	
15	رَسُوْلٍ كَرِيْمٍ		
16			الطَّالِبَاتُ الشَّاكِرَاتُ

Education | Preservation | Application

Vocabulary Crosswords

QURAN

English to Arabic:

DOWN	ACROSS
3. souls	1. gratitude
6. reckoning	2. sadness (p)
9. set time period	4. rejection
10. transgression	5. misguidance
11. eternity	7. piety
12. filth	8. pure
14. righteousness	13. firmness

Arabic to English:

DOWN	ACROSS
3. إِلَهٌ	1. خَشْيَةٌ
5. حَرَامٌ	2. رَيْبٌ
9. أَبْكَمُ	4. بُخْلٌ
10. ضَعْفُ	6. بَرَّةً
11. أَخْطَاء	7. أَمْرٌ
12. آثَامٌ	8. أَجْرٌ

Mudhaaf and Mudhaaf Ilaih

Mudhaaf and Mudhaaf ilaih

- The مُضَافٌ (word before "of") should be:
    ◊ No Tanween
    ◊ No alif-Laam (ال)
- The مُضَافٌ إِلَيْهِ (word after "of") should always be مَجْرُوْرٌ
- The مَعْرِفَةٌ/نَكِرَةٌ property of مُضَافٌ is dictated by it's مُضَافٌ إِلَيْهِ
- Both مُضَافٌ (first) and مُضَافٌ إِلَيْهِ (second) must be written right after the other (no long distance relationship)
- Both مُضَافٌ إِلَيْهِ and مُضَافٌ must be اِسْم
- In some cases, the phrase means that the second word owns or possess the first
- The إِعْرَابٌ of the مُضَافٌ will be according to the عَامِلٌ governing it and that will be considered the status of the whole phrase
- Sometimes many مُضَافٌ, مُضَافٌ إِلَيْهِ are found in one single phrase
- It is NOT a complete sentence

مُضَاف   مُضَاف إليه

English	Arabic
The servant (f) of the house	خَادِمَةُ الْبَيْتِ
The house of the servant (f)	بَيْتُ الْخَادِمَةِ
The pen of a boy A boy's pen	قَلَمُ وَلَدٍ
The man's book	كِتَابُ الرَّجُلِ
A teacher's house	بَيْتُ مُعَلِّمٍ
The class's board The board of the class	سَبُّوْرَةُ الْفَصْلِ

Mudhaaf and Mudhaaf ilaih

Drill #25

Make the nouns in column A, Mudhaaf and those in column B, the Mudhaaf ilaih

	A	B	Fragment	Translation
1	رَسُوْلٌ	اللهُ		
2	الطَّالِبَاتُ	الْمَدْرَسَةُ		
3	مِفْتَاحٌ	الْبَابَ		
4	حَقِيْبَةٌ	طَالِبٌ		
5	الْمَرَاسِمُ	الْأَسَاتِذَةَ		
6	حِبْرٌ	قَلَمٌ		
7	كُرَّاسَةً	طَالِبَةً		
8	السَّبُّوْرَةُ	الْفَصْلَ		
9	مِمْحَاةً	الْأُسْتَاذُ		
10	شَجْرَةً	الْبُسْتَانَ		
11	غُصْنٌ	شَجْرَةً		
12	وَرَقَةً	غُصْنٌ		
13	نُجُوْمٍ	السَّمَاءَ		
14	الْجُدُرَ	الْمَدْرَسَةُ		
15	الْمَفَاتِيْح	قُفْلٌ		
16	الْمَكَاتِبُ	الطُّلَّابُ		

Mudhaaf and Mudhaaf ilaih

Drill #26

Underline the Mudhaaf and Mudhaaf ilaih fragments

	Ayah
1	سَلَامٌ هِيَ حَتَّىٰ مَطْلَعِ الْفَجْرِ 97:5
2	إِلَّا الَّذِينَ آمَنُوا وَعَمِلُوا الصَّالِحَاتِ فَلَهُمْ أَجْرٌ غَيْرُ مَمْنُونٍ 95:6
3	إِنَّ أَصْحَابَ الْجَنَّةِ الْيَوْمَ فِي شُغُلٍ فَاكِهُونَ 36:55
4	قُلْ إِنَّمَا الْعِلْمُ عِندَ اللَّهِ وَإِنَّمَا أَنَا نَذِيرٌ مُّبِينٌ 67:26
5	رَبُّ الْمَشْرِقَيْنِ وَرَبُّ الْمَغْرِبَيْنِ 55:17
6	وَأَقِيمُوا الصَّلَاةَ وَآتُوا الزَّكَاةَ وَارْكَعُوا مَعَ الرَّاكِعِينَ 2:43
7	نَارُ اللَّهِ الْمُوقَدَةُ 104:6
8	كُلُّ نَفْسٍ ذَائِقَةُ الْمَوْتِ 21:35
9	وَإِذْ نَجَّيْنَاكُم مِّنْ آلِ فِرْعَوْنَ يَسُومُونَكُمْ سُوءَ الْعَذَابِ 2:49
10	إِنَّ الَّذِينَ آمَنُوا وَعَمِلُوا الصَّالِحَاتِ كَانَتْ لَهُمْ جَنَّاتُ الْفِرْدَوْسِ نُزُلًا 18:107
11	وَإِنَّ رَبَّكَ لَذُو مَغْفِرَةٍ لِّلنَّاسِ عَلَىٰ ظُلْمِهِمْ ۖ وَإِنَّ رَبَّكَ لَشَدِيدُ الْعِقَابِ 13:6
12	تَبَارَكَ الَّذِي بِيَدِهِ الْمُلْكُ وَهُوَ عَلَىٰ كُلِّ شَيْءٍ قَدِيرٌ 67:1
13	وَهُمْ يُجَادِلُونَ فِي اللَّهِ وَهُوَ شَدِيدُ الْمِحَالِ 13:13
14	يَا أَيُّهَا النَّاسُ اتَّقُوا رَبَّكُمْ ۚ إِنَّ زَلْزَلَةَ السَّاعَةِ شَيْءٌ عَظِيمٌ 22:1
15	قَالَتِ امْرَأَتُ الْعَزِيزِ الْآنَ حَصْحَصَ الْحَقُّ أَنَا رَاوَدتُّهُ عَن نَّفْسِهِ وَإِنَّهُ لَمِنَ الصَّادِقِينَ 12:51
16	ذَٰلِكُمْ وَأَنَّ اللَّهَ مُوهِنُ كَيْدِ الْكَافِرِينَ 8:18
17	إِنَّ اللَّهَ لَا يَظْلِمُ مِثْقَالَ ذَرَّةٍ ۖ وَإِن تَكُ حَسَنَةً يُضَاعِفْهَا وَيُؤْتِ مِن لَّدُنْهُ أَجْرًا عَظِيمًا 4:40
18	الْحَمْدُ لِلَّهِ رَبِّ الْعَالَمِينَ 1:1
19	اللَّهُ نُورُ السَّمَاوَاتِ وَالْأَرْضِ ۚ مَثَلُ نُورِهِ كَمِشْكَاةٍ فِيهَا مِصْبَاحٌ 24:35
20	صِرَاطَ الَّذِينَ أَنْعَمْتَ عَلَيْهِمْ غَيْرِ الْمَغْضُوبِ عَلَيْهِمْ وَلَا الضَّالِّينَ 1:7

Mudhaaf and Mudhaaf ilaih

Drill #27

Door	بَابٌ	House	بَيْتٌ	Page	وَرَقٌ	Book	كِتَابٌ
Fatima	فَاطِمَةُ	Water	مَاءٌ	Pen	قَلَمٌ	Ocean	بَحْرٌ
Servant	خَادِمٌ	Car	سَيَّارَةٌ	Key	مِفْتَاحٌ	Lock	قُفْلٌ
Window	نَافِذَةٌ	Desk	مَكْتَبٌ	Student	طَالِبٌ	Class	فَصْلٌ
Food	طَعَامٌ	Boy	وَلَدٌ	Board	سَبُّورَةٌ	Muslim	مُسْلِمٌ

Translate the following phrases into Arabic

	English	Arabic		English	Arabic
1.	The door of the house		4.	Water of the ocean	
2.	The page of the book		5.	Servant of the house	
3.	Fatima's pen		6.	Servant's house	

Translate the following phrases into English

	Arabic	English		Arabic	English
1.	بَابُ السَّيَّارَةِ		4.	طَعَامُ الْوَلَدِ	
2.	مِفْتَاحُ النَّافِذَةِ		5.	سَبُّورَةُ الْفَصْلِ	
3.	مَكْتَبُ الْفَصْلِ		6.	بَيْتُ الْمُسْلِمِيْنَ	

Mudhaaf and Mudhaaf ilaih

Drill #28

Form 5 Mudhaff and Mudhaff ilaih fragments using the words in the word bank.

Pencil	مِرْسَمٌ		Car	سَيَّارَةٌ
House	بَيْتٌ		Scholar (F)	عَالِمَةٌ
Key	مِفْتَاحٌ		School	مَدْرَسَةٌ
Student	طَالِبٌ		Girl	بِنْتٌ

	English	Arabic
1		
2		
3		
4		
5		
6		
7		
8		
9		
10		
11		
12		
13		

Vocabulary Crosswords

PEOPLE

English to Arabic:

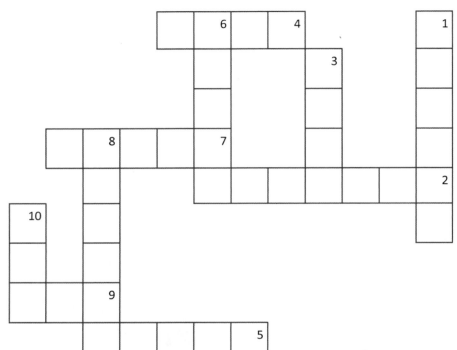

DOWN	ACROSS
1. mothers	2. female cousins
3. grandfathers	4. maternal uncles
6. butcher	5. sons
8. doctors	7. paternal aunt
9. daughter	9. brothers

Arabic to English:

DOWN	ACROSS
4. خَبَّازٌ	1. بَنَاتُ عَمٍّ
6. أُسْتَاذٌ	2. أَصْدِقَاءُ
7. وَلَدٌ	3. أَبٌ
8. نَاتٌ	5. مُجْرِمٌ
9. اِخْوَانٌ	
10. تَلَامِيْذٌ	

Jumla Ismiyyah
Nominal Sentence

Jumla Ismiyyah— Nominal Sentence

- The الْجُمْلَةُ الْاِسْمِيَّةُ is that sentence which begins with an ISM. Jumla Ismiyyah is sentence which is made up of two parts:
    - The first part of the sentence is called مُبْتَدَأ (subject), i.e. the thing you are talking about.
    - The second part is called خَبَرٌ (predicate), the information regarding the subject

The man is truthful

In the above example, the man is the subject and truthful is the predicate (information about the subject)

- **Rules of** مُبْتَدَأ **and** خَبَرٌ

    - The مُبْتَدَأ is given first, followed by the خَبَرٌ .

    - The مُبْتَدَأ must be a noun in the state of رَفْعٌ .

    - The خَبَرٌ must match the مُبْتَدَأ in I'rab, Number and Gender (ING), but not Definite/Indefinite

- **Translation of Jumla Ismiyyah**

    - In Arabic, there is no word for "is" or its variants (am, are), however they must be added to the English translation

English	Arabic خَبَرٌ ← مُبْتَدَأ →
The man is truthful	الرَّجُلُ صَادِقٌ
The men are truthful	الرِّجَالُ صَادِقُوْنَ
The sister is truthful	الْأُخْتُ صَادِقَةٌ
The sisters are truthful	الْأَخَوَاتُ صَادِقَاتٌ

Jumla Ismiyyah— Nominal Sentence

Drill #29

Difficult	صَعْبٌ	Old	قَدِيْمٌ	Skillful	مَاهِرٌ	Honest	أَمِيْنٌ
Easy	سَهْلٌ	New	جَدِيْدٌ	Pious	صَالِحٌ	Merciful	رَحِيْمٌ
Beautiful	جَمِيْلٌ	Tall/Long	طَوِيْلٌ	Generous	كَرِيْمٌ	Big	كَبِيْرٌ
Close	مُغْلَقٌ	Smart	ذَكِيٌّ	Clean	نَظِيْفٌ	Small	صَغِيْرٌ
Open	مَفْتُوْحٌ	Broken	مَكْسُوْرٌ	Dirty	وَسِخٌ	Muslim	مُسْلِمٌ

Fill in the blanks with appropriate predicate from above list and then translate:

Translation	Arabic		Translation	Arabic	
	الشُّبَّاكُ _____	11.		_____ الْقَلَمُ	1.
	الْبَيْتُ _____	12.		_____ السُّلَّمُ	2.
	الْبَابُ _____	13.		_____ الْوَلَدُ	3.
	الْأَبُ _____	14.		_____ خَالِدٌ	4.
	الْإِبْنُ _____	15.		الْكِتَابُ _____	5.
	الْأُسْتَاذُ _____	16.		_____ الْمِرْسَمُ	6.
	الْعَمُّ _____	17.		الْقُفْلُ _____	7.
	_____ الصَّدِيْقُ	18.		_____ الْقِدْرُ	8.
	_____ التِّلْمِيْذُ	19.		_____ الصَّحْنُ	9.
	الزَّوْجُ _____	20.		_____ الْقَمَرُ	10.

Jumla Ismiyyah— Nominal Sentence

Drill #30

Difficult	صَعْبٌ	Old	قَدِيْمٌ	Skillful	مَاهِرٌ	Honest	أَمِيْنٌ
Easy	سَهْلٌ	New	جَدِيْدٌ	Pious	صَالِحٌ	Merciful	رَحِيْمٌ
Beautiful	جَمِيْلٌ	Tall/Long	طَوِيْلٌ	Generous	كَرِيْمٌ	Big	كَبِيْرٌ
Close	مُغْلَقٌ	Smart	ذَكِيٌّ	Clean	نَظِيْفٌ	Small	صَغِيْرٌ
Open	مَفْتُوْحٌ	Broken	مَكْسُوْرٌ	Dirty	وَسِخٌ	Muslim	مُسْلِمٌ

Fill in the blanks with appropriate predicate from above list and then translate:

Translation	Arabic		Translation	Arabic	
	_____ الشَّمْعَةُ	11.		_____ الشَّمْسُ	1.
	_____ الأُخْتُ	12.		_____ النَّافِذَةُ	2.
	_____ الطَّاوِلَةُ	13.		_____ الْبِنْتُ	3.
	الأُمُّ _____	14.		_____ فَاطِمَةُ	4.
	_____ الإِبْنَةُ	15.		_____ الْمَرْأَةُ	5.
	الأُسْتَاذَةُ _____	16.		_____ الْمَغْسَلَةُ	6.
	الْعَمَّةُ _____	17.		_____ الْخَزَانَةُ	7.
	_____ الصَّدِيْقَةُ	18.		_____ السَّجَّادَةُ	8.
	_____ التِّلْمِيْذَةُ	19.		_____ السَّاعَةُ	9.
	الزَّوْجَةُ _____	20.		_____ السِّتَارَةُ	10.

Jumla Ismiyyah— Nominal Sentence

Drill #31

Difficult	صَعْبٌ	Old	قَدِيمٌ	Skillful	مَاهِرٌ	Honest	أَمِينٌ
Easy	سَهْلٌ	New	جَدِيدٌ	Pious	صَالِحٌ	Merciful	رَحِيمٌ
Beautiful	جَمِيلٌ	Tall/Long	طَوِيلٌ	Generous	كَرِيمٌ	Big	كَبِيرٌ
Close	مُغْلَقٌ	Smart	ذَكِيٌّ	Clean	نَظِيفٌ	Small	صَغِيرٌ
Open	مَفْتُوحٌ	Truthful	صَادِقٌ	Dirty	وَسِخٌ	Muslim	مُسْلِمٌ

Fill in the blanks with appropriate predicate from above list and then translate:

Translation	Arabic		Translation	Arabic	
	ــــــــ الْخَادِمَاتُ	11.		ــــــــ الْخَادِمَانِ	1.
	ــــــــ الْوَلَدَانِ	12.		ــــــــ الْأَوْلَادُ	2.
	ــــــــ الْبِنْتَانِ	13.		ــــــــ الْبَنَاتُ	3.
	ــــــــ الْأُمَّهَاتُ	14.		ــــــــ الْمُهَنْدِسُوْنَ	4.
	ــــــــ الْإِبْنَانِ	15.		ــــــــ الْمَرْأَتَانِ	5.
	ــــــــ الْأَخْوَالُ	16.		ــــــــ الْأَصْدِقَاءُ	6.
	ــــــــ الْعَمَّاتُ	17.		ــــــــ الْأُسْتَاذَانِ	7.
	ــــــــ الْمُجْرِمَتَانِ	18.		ــــــــ التَّلَامِيْذُ	8.
	ــــــــ الْخَبَّازُوْنَ	19.		ــــــــ الْمُجْرِمُوْنَ	9.
	ــــــــ الزَّوْجَاتُ	20.		ــــــــ الطَّبِيْبَانِ	10.

Jumla Ismiyyah— Nominal Sentence

Drill #32

Correct the grammatical errors in the following sentences:

	Sentence	Corrected		Sentence	Corrected
1	الطَّالِبَةُ عِرَاقِيَّةٌ		17	سَجَّادَةٌ اِيْرَانِيٌّ	
2	مُعَلِّمُ الْحَاضِرُوْنَ		18	الطِّفْلَيْنِ ضَاحِكَيْنِ	
3	الدَّوْلَابُ مُغْلَقَةٌ		19	طِفْلٍ صَغِيْرٍ	
4	الْبِنْتُ جَمِيْلٌ		20	الزَّوْجَةُ الصَّالِحَةَ	
5	الْمُسَافِرِيْنَ رَاجِعِيْنَ		21	الصُّنْدُوْقِ الْقَدِيْمِ	
6	الْبَيْتُ كَبِيْرَةٌ		22	خَادِمَةٌ أَمِيْنًا	
7	الطَّالِبَانِ ذَكِيٌّ		23	فَاطِمَةُ طَبِيْبٌ	
8	الْمُهَنْدِسُوْنَ مَاهِرًا		24	الْمُنَافِقِيْنَ كَثِيْرُوْنَ	
9	الأَبُ مُجْتَهِدٌ		25	وَرْدَتَيْنِ جَمِيْلَتَيْنِ	
10	دَرْسُ صَعْبٌ		26	بَقَرَةٌ صَفْرَاءُ	
11	زَيْدٍ طَبِيْبٌ		27	صَالِحَةٌ تَقِيَّةً	
12	فَتَاتَانِ مُهَذَّبَةٌ		28	بَابَانِ مَفْتُوْحٌ	
13	الْمُسْلِمَاتُ شَاكِرَاتٌ		29	الرِّجَالُ الْكَرِيْمُ	
14	طُلَّابٌ مَسْرُوْرِيْنَ		30	الْوَلَدَيْنِ صَغِيْرَيْنِ	
15	أُمُّ الصَّادِقَةُ		31	الْحَدِيْقَةِ الْوَاسِعَةِ	
16	لُغَةُ سَهْلٌ		32	الْبُسْتَانُ جَمِيْلٌ	

Jumla Ismiyyah— Nominal Sentence

Drill #33

Difficult	صَعْبٌ	Old	قَدِيْمٌ	Skillful	مَاهِرٌ	Truthful	صَادِقٌ
Easy	سَهْلٌ	New	جَدِيْدٌ	Pious	صَالِحٌ	Merciful	رَحِيْمٌ
Beautiful	جَمِيْلٌ	Tall/Long	طَوِيْلٌ	Generous	كَرِيْمٌ	Big	كَبِيْرٌ
Open	مَفْتُوْحٌ	Muslim	مُسْلِمٌ	Clean	نَظِيْفٌ	Small	صَغِيْرٌ

Translate the following sentences into Arabic and vice versa:

	English	Arabic		English	Arabic
1.	The Masjid is beautiful		16.	The chair is big	
2.	The mothers are pious		17.	The door is clean	
3.	The boys are truthful		18.	The school is open	
4.	The doctors (f) are generous		19.	The teachers (f) are generous	
5.	The door is new		20.	The girl is small	
6.	The house is clean		21.	The men are Muslims	
7.	Sisters(2) are Muslims		22.	The lesson is easy	
8.	The uncle is tall		23.	The girls are Muslims	
9.	The lesson is difficult		24.	The door is beautiful	
10.	The teacher (f) is new		25.	The students are tall	
11.	The teachers (2) are skillful		26.	The Muslims(2) are new	
12.	The students (f) are generous		27.	The friends (2) are truthful	
13.	The Masjids (2) are old		28.	The doctors are old	
14.	The Muslims are truthful		29.	The mouth is open	
15.	The eyes are beautiful		30.	The kitchen is clean	

Jumla Ismiyyah— Nominal Sentence

Drill #34

Translate the following sentences into Arabic and vice versa:

	English	Arabic		English	Arabic
1	The boy is in the Masjid		1		مِفْتَاحُ الْبَابِ صَغِيرٌ
2	The keys are on the car		2		يَدُ الطِّفْلِ وَسِخَةٌ
3	The girl is with the father		3		ثَمَرَاتِ الشَّجْرَةِ نَظِيفٌ
4	The uncle is from Canada		4		الْقَمَرُ الْجَمِيلُ فِي السَّمَاءِ
5	The car is for the teacher		5		نَافِذَةُ الْبَيْتِ مَفْتُوحَةٌ
6	The big door is broken		6		دَرْسُ الْمُعَلِّمَةِ سَهْلٌ
7	The new students are hardworking		7		مَرْيَمُ مُعَلِّمَةٌ جَيِّدَةٌ
8	The beautiful garden is small		8		اَلسَّيَّارَةُ الْجَدِيدَةُ سَرِيعَةٌ
9	The pious wife is a blessing from Allah		9		اَلْغُرْفَةُ الْكَبِيرَةُ وَسِخَةٌ
10	Khalid is a strong man		10		اَلْمَرْأَةُ أُسْتَاذَةٌ مَشْهُورَةٌ
11	The cold water is in the refrigerator		11		اَلطَّبَّاخَةُ الذَّكِيَّةُ حَزِينَةٌ
12	Zaid's book is on the desk		12		عَائِشَةُ مِنَ الْمِصْرِ
13	The pen's ink is black		13		الْكِتَابُ عَنْ أَمْرِيكَا
14	Zaid's daughters are generous		14		اَلدَّكْتُورَةُ الْجَدِيدَةُ امْرَأَةٌ طَوِيلَةٌ
15	Students of the school are hardworking		15		خَالِدٌ لَاعِبٌ عَرَبِيٌّ مُمْتَازٌ
16	The woman's daughter is a smart girl		16		اَلنَّجَاحُ لِلْمُجْتَهِدِينَ

Inna and Her Sisters

Inna and Her Sisters

Drill #35

Huroof Nasb						
لَعَلَّ	لُكِنَّ	لَيْتَ	بِأَنَّ	كَأَنَّ	أَنَّ	إِنَّ
So that, hopefully, maybe, perhaps	However, but	Alas (express regret)	because	As though, as if	that	Certainly, indeed

When you have learnt the Huroof Nasb chart please find 3 different people in your class to sign off your charts and after that read it to the instructor/TA for final sign off

Huroof Nasb Chart—Memorization Tracker				
Particle	Person 1	Person 2	Person 3	Instructor/TA
Huroof Nasb				

	Aayah Fragments	**Harf Nasb**	**Mansoob**
1	ذَلِكَ بِأَنَّ اللَّهَ نَزَّلَ الْكِتَابَ بِالْحَقّ – 2:176		
2	إِنَّ الْكَافِرِينَ كَانُوا لَكُمْ عَدُوًّا مُّبِينًا – 4:101		
3	قِيلَ ادْخُلِ الْجَنَّةَ ۖ قَالَ يَا لَيْتَ قَوْمِي يَعْلَمُونَ – 36:26		
4	وَمَا يُدْرِيكَ لَعَلَّ السَّاعَةَ قَرِيبٌ – 42:17		
5	وَيَقُولُ يَا لَيْتَنِي لَمْ أُشْرِكْ بِرَبِّي أَحَدًا – 18:42		
6	لَعَلَّ اللَّهَ يُحْدِثُ بَعْدَ ذَٰلِكَ أَمْرًا – 65:1		
7	وَأَنَّ الْمَسَاجِدَ لِلَّهِ فَلَا تَدْعُوا مَعَ اللَّهِ أَحَدًا – 72:18		
8	إِنَّ فِي السَّمَاوَاتِ وَالْأَرْضِ لَآيَاتٍ لِّلْمُؤْمِنِينَ – 45:3		
9	وَإِذَا تُتْلَىٰ عَلَيْهِ آيَاتُنَا وَلَّىٰ مُسْتَكْبِرًا كَأَن لَّمْ يَسْمَعْهَا كَأَنَّ فِي أُذُنَيْهِ وَقْرًا – 31:7		
10	أَنَّ لَهُمْ أَجْرًا كَبِيرًا – 17:9		
11	إِنَّ اللَّهَ عَلَىٰ كُلِّ شَىْءٍ قَدِيرٌ – 2:20		
12	إِنَّ الصَّفَا وَالْمَرْوَةَ مِن شَعَائِرِ اللَّهِ – 2:185		
13	وَمَا أُنزِلَ إِلَيْهِ مَا اتَّخَذُوهُمْ أَوْلِيَاءَ وَلَٰكِنَّ كَثِيرًا مِّنْهُمْ فَاسِقُونَ – 5:81		
14	يَا أَيُّهَا النَّاسُ اتَّقُوا رَبَّكُمْ إِنَّ زَلْزَلَةَ السَّاعَةِ شَيْءٌ عَظِيمٌ – 22:1		
15	إِنَّ الْحَسَنَاتِ يُذْهِبْنَ السَّيِّئَاتِ ۚ ذَٰلِكَ ذِكْرَىٰ لِلذَّاكِرِينَ – 11:114		

Inna and Her Sisters

Drill #36

Adding the particle to the sentence, write the updated sentence

	Sentence	Particle	New sentence
1	الصَّدِيْقَانِ جَدِيْدَانِ	إِنَّ	
2	الْفَتَايَاتُ مُهَذَّبَاتٌ	إِنَّ	
3	الْحُجَّاجُ قَادِمُوْنَ	لَعَلَّ	
4	الْبِنْتُ جَمِيْلَةٌ	إِنَّ	
5	الْأُمَّهَاتُ مُؤْمِنَاتٌ	إِنَّ	
6	الْبَيْتُ كَبِيْرٌ	إِنَّ	
7	الْمُعَلِّمُوْنَ آبَاءٌ	كَأَنَّ	
8	الْمُهَنْدِسُوْنَ مَاهِرٌ	إِنَّ	
9	الْأَبُ مُجْتَهِدٌ	إِنَّ	
10	الْأَخَوَانِ صَالِحَانِ	لَعَلَّ	
11	الامْتِحَانُ سَهْلٌ	لَعَلَّ	
12	الْأَرْضُ كُرَّةٌ	كَأَنَّ	
13	السَّعَادَةُ دَائِمَةٌ	لَيْتَ	
14	الطُّلَّابُ مَسْرُوْرُوْنَ	إِنَّ	
15	الْأُمُّ صَادِقَةٌ	إِنَّ	
16	الْعَرَبِيَّةُ سَهْلَةٌ	لَعَلَّ	
17	الْأَسَاتِذَةُ مُخْلِصُوْنَ	إِنَّ	
18	الْمَرِيْضُ مُعَالَجٌ	لَعَلَّ	
19	الْأَوْلَادُ مُسْلِمُوْنَ	إِنَّ	
20	الْمُجَاهِدُوْنَ مُنْتَصِرُوْنَ	لَعَلَّ	

Review

Drill #37

Explain all the rules in the order of hardest to easiest in your opinion. Then review it with another student in your class and get him/her sign this page.

Vocabulary Crosswords

BODY PARTS— LOCATIONS

English to Arabic:

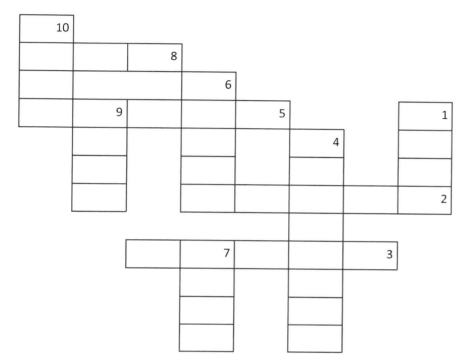

DOWN	ACROSS
1. restaurants	2. library
4. hospital	3. mouths
6. tongues	5. play grounds
7. hands	8. foot
9. eyes	
10. hearts	

Arabic to English:

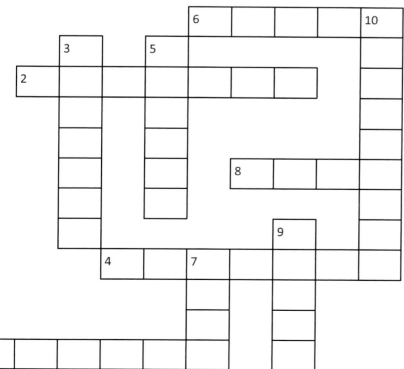

DOWN	ACROSS
3. مَطَارٌ	1. لِسَانٌ
5. مَدْرَسَةٌ	2. مَطْبَخٌ
7. أَنْفٌ	4. أَصَابِعُ
9. رُئُوْسٌ	6. فَمٌ
10. مُسْتَشْفَيَاتٌ	8. أَرْجُلٌ

Prounouns

Attached and Unattached Pronouns

Drill #38

Plural	جمع	Dual	تثنية	Singular	واحد	
Detached Pronouns						
They	هُمْ	They (2)	هُمَا	He	هُوَ	3rd M
They (F)	هُنَّ	They (2)(F)	هُمَا	She	هِىَ	3rd F
You (all)	اَنْتُمْ	You (2)	اَنْتُمَا	You	اَنْتَ	2nd M
You (all) (F)	اَنْتُنَّ	You (2)(F)	اَنْتُمَا	You (F)	اَنْتِ	2nd F
We		نَحْنُ		I	اَنَا	1st

Plural	جمع	Dual	تثنية	Singular	واحد	
Attached Pronouns with Nouns						
Their	هُمْ – هِمْ	Their (2)	هُمَا – هِمَا	His	هُ – هِ	3rd M
Their (F)	هُنَّ – هِنَّ	Their (2)(F)	هُمَا – هِمَا	Her	هَا	3rd F
Your (all)	كُمْ	Your (2)	كُمَا	Your	كَ	2nd M
Your (all) (F)	كُنَّ	Your (2)(F)	كُمَا	Your (F)	كِ	2nd F
Our		نَا		My	ي	1st

When you have learnt the above charts please find 3 different people in your class to sign off your charts and after that read it to the instructor/TA for final sign off

Pronoun Charts—Memorization Tracker

Pronoun	Person 1	Person 2	Person 3	Instructor/TA
Detached				
Attached				

Attached and Unattached Pronouns

Drill #39

Translate the following phrases into Arabic and vice versa:

	English	Arabic		English	Arabic
1.	He is a boy		1.		أَنْتُمَا طَالِبَتَانِ
2.	She is a mother		2.		أَنَا رَجُلٌ
3.	I am a student (f)		3.		أَنْتَ تِلْمِيْذٌ
4.	We are Muslims		4.		نَحْنُ أَخَوَاتٌ
5.	They are brothers		5.		هِيَ بِنْتٌ
6.	You (f) are a doctor		6.		أَنْتُنَّ صَادِقَاتٌ
7.	You (all) are generous		7.		هُمَا صَدِيْقَانِ
8.	They (f) are pious		8.		أَنْتُمْ مُجْرِمُوْنَ
9.	She is Fatima		9.		هُنَّ مُجْتَهِدُوْنَ
10.	They are Hamza and Fatima		10.		أَنْتِ مُسْلِمَةٌ
11.	You are Khalid		11.		هُمْ أَصْدِقَاءُ
12.	You (2) are pious		12.		أَنْتُمَا كَرِيْمَانِ
13.	You are Laila and Warda		13.		هُمَا خُبَّازَتَانِ
14.	You(all)(f) are in the car		14.		هِيَ كَسَيَّارَةٍ
15.	I am from Canada		15.		أَنْتَ مِنَ الْبَاكِسْتَانِ
16.	They (f) are like sisters		16.		هُوَ مَكْتَبٌ

Attached and Detached Pronouns

Drill #40

Complete the charts

Plural	جمع	Dual	تثنية	Singular	واحد	
			كِتَابُهُمَا	His book	كِتَابُهُ	3rd M
	كِتَابُهُنَّ					3rd F
					كِتَابُكَ	2nd M
	كِتَابُكُنَّ		كِتَابُكُمَا			2nd F
Our book					كِتَابِيْ	1st

Attached Pronouns in action

Plural	جمع	Dual	تثنية	Singular	واحد	
					قَلَمَهُ	3rd M
						3rd F
						2nd M
						2nd F
						1st

Attached and Unattached Pronouns

Drill #41

Translate the following phrases into Arabic and vice versa:

	English	Arabic		English	Arabic
1.	Our Masjid		1.		أُخْتُكُمْ
2.	His sisters		2.		أَبُوكُمَا
3.	My pillow		3.		وَلَدُهُمَا
4.	Her chair		4.		مَسْجِدِي
5.	Their school		5.		كُرْسِيُّهُ
6.	Your refrigerator		6.		خَبَّازُنَا
7.	Their (2) desk		7.		سَبِيلُكَ
8.	Your (f) spoon		8.		شَوْكَتُهَا
9.	Their (f) table		9.		صَحْنِي
10.	Your (all) (f) keys		10.		شُبَّاكُهُمْ
11.	Your (all) home		11.		عَمُّهُ
12.	Your (2) garden		12.		خَزَانَاتُكُمْ
13.	My eraser		13.		مِرْآةُهُنَّ
14.	Our blackboard		14.		فُرُشُكُنَّ
15.	Your sharpener		15.		مِذْيَاعُهُمَا
16.	Their bags		16.		مَكَاتِبُكُمَا

Attached and Unattached Pronouns

Drill #42

	جمع	Plural		تثنية	Dual	Singular		واحد	

Plural	جمع	Dual	تثنية	Singular	واحد	
	لَهُمْ		لَهُمَا	for him/it	لَهُ	3rd M
	لَهُنَّ		لَهُمَا		لَهَا	3rd F
	لَكُمْ		لَكُمَا		لَكَ	2nd M
	لَكُنَّ		لَكُمَا		لَكِ	2nd F
		لَنَا			لِي	1st

Attached Pronouns with Huroof Jarr

Plural	جمع	Dual	تثنية	Singular	واحد	
				from him/it	مِنْهُ	3rd M
						3rd F
						2nd M
						2nd F
		مِنَّا			مِنِّي	1st

Attached Pronouns with Huroof Jarr

Plural	جمع	Dual	تثنية	Singular	واحد	
	فِيْهِمْ		فِيْهِمَا	In him/it	فِيْهِ	3rd M
	فِيْهِنَّ		فِيْهِمَا			3rd F
						2nd M
						2nd F
In/among us		فِيْنَا			فِيَّ	1st

Attached and Unattached Pronouns

Drill #43

Plural	جمع	Dual	تثنية	Singular	واحد	
						Attached Pronouns with Huroof Jarr
	بِهِمْ		بِهِمَا	with him/it	بِهِ	3rd M
	بِهِنَّ		بِهِمَا			3rd F
						2nd M
						2nd F
		بِنَا			بِي	1st

Plural	جمع	Dual	تثنية	Singular	واحد	
						Attached Pronouns with Huroof Jarr
	عَلَيْهِمْ		عَلَيْهِمَا	upon him/it	عَلَيْهِ	3rd M
	عَلَيْهِنَّ		عَلَيْهِمَا			3rd F
						2nd M
						2nd F
		عَلَيْنَا			عَلَيَّ	1st

Plural	جمع	Dual	تثنية	Singular	واحد	
						Attached Pronouns with Huroof Jarr
	إِلَيْهِمْ		إِلَيْهِمَا		إِلَيْهِ	3rd M
	إِلَيْهِنَّ		إِلَيْهِمَا			3rd F
						2nd M
						2nd F
To/towards us		إِلَيْنَا			إِلَيَّ	1st

Attached and Unattached Pronouns

Drill #44

		Singular	تثنية	Dual	جمع	Plural
		Attached Pronouns with Huroof Nasb				
Plural	جمع	Dual	تثنية	Singular	واحد	
3rd M	إِنَّهُ	Indeed he/it	إِنَّهُمَا			
3rd F			إِنَّهُمَا			
2nd M						
2nd F						
1st	إِنِّي — إِنَّنِي		إِنَّا — إِنَّنَا			Indeed we

		Attached Pronouns with Huroof Nasb				
Plural	جمع	Dual	تثنية	Singular	واحد	
3rd M	لَعَلَّهُ	That he might				
3rd F						
2nd M						
2nd F						
1st	لَعَلِّي		لَعَلَّنَا			

		Attached Pronouns with Huroof Nasb				
Plural	جمع	Dual	تثنية	Singular	واحد	
3rd M	لَيْتَهُ					
3rd F						
2nd M						
2nd F						
1st	لَيْتَنِيْ		لَيْتَنَا			

Attached and Detached Pronouns

Drill #45

Circle the pronouns and write their meaning

Meaning	Ayah
	1 هُوَ الَّذِي خَلَقَ لَكُم مَّا فِي الْأَرْضِ جَمِيعًا 2:29
	2 وَالَّذِينَ يُؤْمِنُونَ بِمَا أُنزِلَ إِلَيْكَ وَمَا أُنزِلَ مِن قَبْلِكَ وَبِالْآخِرَةِ هُمْ يُوقِنُونَ 2:4
	3 وَاتْلُ عَلَيْهِمْ نَبَأَ ابْنَيْ آدَمَ بِالْحَقِّ إِذْ قَرَّبَا قُرْبَانًا فَتُقُبِّلَ مِنْ أَحَدِهِمَا 5:27
	4 فِي قُلُوبِهِم مَّرَضٌ فَزَادَهُمُ اللَّهُ مَرَضًا ۖ وَلَهُمْ عَذَابٌ أَلِيمٌ بِمَا كَانُوا يَكْذِبُونَ 2:10
	5 قَالُوا إِنْ أَنتُمْ إِلَّا بَشَرٌ مِّثْلُنَا 14:10
	6 يُذَبِّحُونَ أَبْنَاءَكُمْ وَيَسْتَحْيُونَ نِسَاءَكُمْ ۚ وَفِي ذَٰلِكُم بَلَاءٌ مِّن رَّبِّكُمْ عَظِيمٌ 2:49
	7 وَإِذْ قَالَ مُوسَىٰ لِقَوْمِهِ يَا قَوْمِ إِنَّكُمْ ظَلَمْتُمْ أَنفُسَكُم بِاتِّخَاذِكُمُ الْعِجْلَ 2:54
	8 قَالُوا تَاللَّهِ إِنَّكَ لَفِي ضَلَالِكَ الْقَدِيمِ 12:95
	9 وَإِذَا سَأَلَكَ عِبَادِي عَنِّي فَإِنِّي قَرِيبٌ 2:186
	10 أَوْ كَالَّذِي مَرَّ عَلَىٰ قَرْيَةٍ وَهِيَ خَاوِيَةٌ عَلَىٰ عُرُوشِهَا 2:259
	11 وَإِذْ قَالَ رَبُّكَ لِلْمَلَائِكَةِ إِنِّي جَاعِلٌ فِي الْأَرْضِ خَلِيفَةً 2:30
	12 حِلَّ لَكُمْ لَيْلَةَ الصِّيَامِ الرَّفَثُ إِلَىٰ نِسَائِكُمْ ۚ هُنَّ لِبَاسٌ لَّكُمْ وَأَنتُمْ لِبَاسٌ لَّهُنَّ 2:187
	13 وَصَدَّقَتْ بِكَلِمَاتِ رَبِّهَا وَكُتُبِهِ وَكَانَتْ مِنَ الْقَانِتِينَ 66:12
	14 مَا خَلَقَ اللَّهُ فِي أَرْحَامِهِنَّ إِن كُنَّ يُؤْمِنَّ بِاللَّهِ وَالْيَوْمِ الْآخِرِ 105:5
	15 فَلَمَّا رَأَىٰ قَمِيصَهُ قُدَّ مِن دُبُرٍ قَالَ إِنَّهُ مِن كَيْدِكُنَّ ۖ إِنَّ كَيْدَكُنَّ عَظِيمٌ 12:28
	16 يُوسُفُ أَعْرِضْ عَنْ هَٰذَا ۚ وَاسْتَغْفِرِي لِذَنبِكِ ۖ إِنَّكِ كُنتِ مِنَ الْخَاطِئِينَ 12:29
	17 أَن تَبَوَّآ لِقَوْمِكُمَا بِمِصْرَ بُيُوتًا وَاجْعَلُوا بُيُوتَكُمْ قِبْلَةً وَأَقِيمُوا الصَّلَاةَ 10:87
	18 الَّذِينَ هُمْ عَن صَلَاتِهِمْ سَاهُونَ 107:5
	19 ضَرَبَ اللَّهُ مَثَلًا كَلِمَةً طَيِّبَةً كَشَجَرَةٍ طَيِّبَةٍ أَصْلُهَا ثَابِتٌ وَفَرْعُهَا فِي السَّمَاءِ 14:24
	20 قَالَتْ لَهُمْ رُسُلُهُمْ إِن نَّحْنُ إِلَّا بَشَرٌ مِّثْلُكُمْ 14:11

Vocabulary Crosswords

CLOTHES—FOOD

English to Arabic:

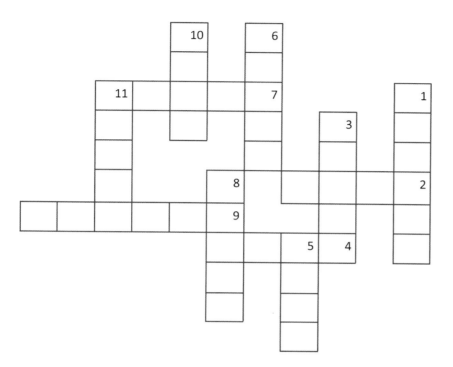

DOWN	ACROSS
1. dresses	2. dates
3. pant	4. meats
5. shoe	7. breads
6. socks	9. caps
8. shirts	
10. long gar-ments	
11. olive	

Arabic to English:

DOWN	ACROSS
1. مِلْحُ	2. جِلْبَابُ
5. خُضَارَةُ	3. تَمْرَةُ
8. سَرَاوِيْلُ	4. قَلَنْسِوَةُ
10. فُسْتَانُ	6. تُفَّاحُ
	7. أَطْعِمَةُ
	9. أَحْذِيَةُ

Review

Drill #46

Identify the Raf, Nasb and Jarr in the following English sentences:

	Sentences	Rafa'	Nasb	Jar
1	The student went to the new library with his brother.			
2	I ate some ice cream after dinner quickly.			
3	She spoke on the phone with her boss.			
4	The car went fast on the highway.			
5	Someone ate my ice cream!!			
6	Abdul hit Zaid harshly.			
7	We visited Chicago to see my family.			
8	The teacher warned the student for misbehaving.			
9	The baby was laughing loudly.			
10	Samia laughed at the funny movie.			
11	The children played at the beach.			
12	Rida bakes delicious cakes.			
13	We learnt Iraab today.			
14	It snowed heavily in Michigan during winter.			
15	She met Hajer's mother at the masjid.			

Review

Accumulative practice:

	Arabic	Type		Arabic	Type
1	آيَاتِ اللهِ		16	مَجْمَعَ الْبَحْرَيْنِ	
2	سِحْرٌ مُبِيْنٌ		17	عَمَلًا صَالِحًا	
3	اَلْبَابُ مَفْتُوْحٌ		18	وَ أَذَانٌ مِنَ اللهِ	
4	كُلِّ مَثَلٍ		19	مَعَ اللهِ	
5	أَنَّ أَصْحَابَ الْجَنَّةِ		20	عِبَادِيْ	
6	كَلِمَةً طَيِّبَةً		21	خَلَقَ السَّمَاوَاتِ	
7	مَنَعَ النَّاسَ		22	جَنَّاتُ عَدْنٍ	
8	أَنَّ وَعْدَ اللهِ		23	الْبَاقِيَاتُ الصَّالِحَاتُ	
9	بَيْتُ اللهِ		24	رَبُّ السَّمَاوَاتِ	
10	قُرْءَانًا عَرَبِيَّةً		25	جَمَعَ مَالًا	
11	يَوْمَ الْحَجِّ		26	هِىَ نَافِذَةُ الْغُرْفَةِ	
12	هُوَ اللهُ		27	مِنَ اللهِ	
13	إِلَى اللهِ		28	سُرُرٌ مَرْفُوْعَةٌ	
14	مَثَلًا رَجُلَيْنِ		29	اَلْمَكْتَبُ مَكْسُوْرٌ	
15	اَلْأَخَوَانِ طَوِيْلَانِ		30	طَعَام الْمِسْكِيْنِ	

Review

Drill #48

Statement	True or False	Corrected Statement, if false
The ism of inna is always majroor		
Mudhaf ileah is always majroor		
Mudhaf sometimes can have tanween		
Two properties of Ism matches in a Mowsoof Siffa phrase		
There are 3 kinds of Iraab (Status) for Ism		
Mudhaf is the possesor		
The Khabar of Inna is mansoob		
Harf Jarr can come before a Fa'el (Verb)		
The state of attached pronoun is Rafa'		

Arabic Morphology (Sarf)

Important Terms

English	عربي
Past	الْمَاضِى
Present	الْمُضَارِع
Imperative	الْأَمْر
3rd Person	غَائِب
2nd Person	حَاضِر
1st Person	مُتَكَلِّم
Feminine	مُؤَنَّث
Masculine	مُذَكَّر
Singular	وَاحِد
Dual	تَثْنِيَة
Plural	جَمْع

Past/Present Tense Vocab Chart

Meaning	Present	Past	Meaning	Present	Past
To create (184)	يَخْلُقُ	خَلَقَ	To take/seize (127)	يَأْخُذُ	أَخَذَ
To enter (76)	يَدْخُلُ	دَخَلَ	To eat (93)	يَأْكُلُ	أَكَلَ
To study (5)	يَدْرُسُ	دَرَسَ	To order/command (77)	يَأْمُرُ	أَمَرَ
To remember (84)	يَذْكُرُ	ذَكَرَ	To reach (40)	يَبْلُغُ	بَلَغَ
To go (45)	يَذْهَبُ	ذَهَبَ	To see (2)	يَبْصُرُ	بَصَرَ
To return (79)	يَرْجِعُ	رَجَعَ	To send (52)	يَبْعَثُ	بَعَثَ
To provide (61)	يَرْزُقُ	رَزَقَ	To leave (40)	يَتْرُكَ	تَرَكَ
To raise (21)	يَرْفَعُ	رَفَعَ	To be established/Firm (1)	يَثْبُتُ	ثَبَتَ
To ride (9)	يَرْكَبُ	رَكِبَ	To come (278)	يَجِيْءُ	جَاءَ
To hear/listen (78)	يَسْمَعُ	سَمِعَ	To make (340)	يَجْعَلُ	جَعَلَ
To question/ask (106)	يَسْئَلُ	سَأَلَ	To sit	يَجْلِسُ	جَلَسَ
To drink (15)	يَشْرَبُ	شَرِبَ	To judge (45)	يَحْكُمُ	حَكَمَ
To thank/be grateful (46)	يَشْكُرُ	شَكَرَ	To calculate/think (44)	يَحْسِبُ	حَسِبَ
To bear witness/testify (44)	يَشْهَدُ	شَهِدَ	To carry/bear (41)	يَحْمِلُ	حَمَلَ
To be patient/bound (58)	يَصْبِرُ	صَبَرَ	To go out/depart (53)	يَخْرُجُ	خَرَجَ

Past/Present Tense Vocab Chart

Meaning	Present	Past	Meaning	Present	Past
To write (49)	يَكْتُبُ	كَتَبَ	To strike/set forth (55)	يَضْرِبُ	ضَرَبَ
To lie (9)	يَكْذِبُ	كَذَبَ	To oppress/ wrong (110)	يَظْلِمُ	ظَلَمَ
To be/become noble	يَكْرُمُ	كَرُمَ	To worship (122)	يَعْبُدُ	عَبَدَ
To earn (62)	يَكْسِبُ	كَسَبَ	To be thirsty	يَعْطَشُ	عَطِشَ
To break	يَكْسِرُ	كَسَرَ	To reason/ understand (49)	يَعْقِلُ	عَقَلَ
To disbelieve (289)	يَكْفِرُ	كَفَرَ	To know (382)	يَعْلَمُ	عَلِمَ
To play (9)	يَلْعَبُ	لَعِبَ	To work/do (276)	يَعْمَلُ	عَمِلَ
To practice	يُمَارِسُ	مَارَسَ	To forgive (65)	يَغْفِرُ	غَفَرَ
To refuse (12)	يَمْنَعُ	مَنَعَ	To open (16)	يَفْتَحُ	فَتَحَ
To make vow (29)	يَنْذُرُ	نَذَرَ	To sin (10)	يَفْسُقُ	فَسَقَ
To help (59)	يَنْصُرُ	نَصَرَ	To do (88)	يَفْعَلُ	فَعَلَ
To watch/view (87)	يَنْظُرُ	نَظَرَ	To say (1618)	يَقُوْلُ	قَالَ
To find (106)	يَجِدُ	وَجَدَ	To stand (26)	يَقُوْمُ	قَامَ
To promise (70)	يَعِدُ	وَعَدَ	To kill (83)	يَقْتُلُ	قَتَلَ

Past Tense Verbs

Past Tense

فِعْل مَاضِي

Plural	جمع		Dual	تثنية		Singular	واحد		
They helped	نَصَرُوْا	هُمْ	They(2) helped	نَصَرَا	هُمَا	He helped	نَصَرَ	هُوَ	3rd M
They(F) helped	نَصَرْنَ	هُنَّ	They(2)(F) helped	نَصَرَتَا	هُمَا	She helped	نَصَرَتْ	هِيَ	3rd F
You(all) helped	نَصَرْتُمْ	اَنْتُمْ	You(2) helped	نَصَرْتُمَا	اَنْتُمَا	You helped	نَصَرْتَ	اَنْتَ	2nd M
You(all)(F) helped	نَصَرْتُنَّ	اَنْتُنَّ	You(2)(F) helped	نَصَرْتُمَا	اَنْتُمَا	You(F) helped	نَصَرْتِ	اَنْتِ	2nd F
We helped			نَصَرْنَا	نَحْنُ		I helped	نَصَرْتُ	اَنَا	1st

Try some oral drills:

ح م ل	ب ل غ	ف ت ح	ر ز ق	أ ك ل	ف ع ل	أ خ ذ	ع ل م	ذ ه ب	ذ ك ر

When you have learnt the Past Tense charts please find 3 different people in your class to sign off your charts and after that read it to the instructor/TA for final sign off

Past Tense Chart—Memorization Tracker				
Verb	Person 1	Person 2	Person 3	Instructor/TA
فِعْل مَاضِي				

Tip: Negating in the past tense: Use the harf مَا

Past Tense Practice Charts

Drill #1

Plural جَمْعٌ			Dual مُثَنَّى			Singular مُفْرَدٌ		
	هُمْ			هُمَا			هُوَ	3rd
	هُنَّ			هُمَا			هِيَ	3rd
	أَنْتُمْ			أَنْتُمَا			أَنْتَ	2nd
	أَنْتُنَّ			أَنْتُمَا			أَنْتِ	2nd
				نَحْنُ			أَنَا	1st

Plural جَمْعٌ			Dual مُثَنَّى			Singular مُفْرَدٌ		
	هُمْ			هُمَا			هُوَ	3rd
	هُنَّ			هُمَا			هِيَ	3rd
	أَنْتُمْ			أَنْتُمَا			أَنْتَ	2nd
	أَنْتُنَّ			أَنْتُمَا			أَنْتِ	2nd
				نَحْنُ			أَنَا	1st

Plural جَمْعٌ			Dual مُثَنَّى			Singular مُفْرَدٌ		
	هُمْ			هُمَا			هُوَ	3rd
	هُنَّ			هُمَا			هِيَ	3rd
	أَنْتُمْ			أَنْتُمَا			أَنْتَ	2nd
	أَنْتُنَّ			أَنْتُمَا			أَنْتِ	2nd
				نَحْنُ			أَنَا	1st

Past Tense Translation Practice

Drill #2

Translate the following words into English and state the pronoun within each Fi'l.

	Arabic word	English Translation	Pronoun		Arabic Word	English Translation	Pronoun
1	نَصَرْتُمْ			19	كَرُمَتَا		
2	نَصَرَ			20	ذَهَبْتِ		
3	بَلَغَتْ			21	فَعَلْتُمْ		
4	قَتَلَا			22	ذَكَرَتْ		
5	نَذَرْنَ			23	ضَرَبْتِ		
6	أَمَرَتَا			24	كَفَرْنَ		
7	مَاكَتَبْتُمَا			25	أَمَرْتُمْ		
8	كَسَبَا			26	رَفَعْتُمَا		
9	مَاخَلَقُوْا			27	مَاجَعَلَا		
10	نَصَرْنَ			28	فَعَلْتُنَّ		
11	أَخَذَتْ			29	قَتَلَتَا		
12	مَاكَفَرْنَ			30	مَافَعَلْتِ		
13	صَبَرُوْا			31	مَنَعَا		
14	مَنَعْتُمْ			32	أَخَذْتُمَا		
15	خَرَجْتُنَّ			33	مَاكَذَبْنَا		
16	مَانَصَرْتُنَّ			34	بَلَغُوْا		
17	عَلِمَ			35	شَكَرَتَا		
18	تَرَكَا			36	عَمِلْتُ		

Past Tense Arabic Translation Practice

Drill #3

Translate the following words into Arabic and state the doer inside each Fi'l.

	English word	Arabic translation	Pronoun		English word	Arabic translation	Pronoun
1	You all (m) helped			21	Both of them testified		
2	They (f) refused			22	We did not forgive		
3	He departed			23	They (f) opened		
4	Both of them (f) drank			24	They made		
5	She disbelieved			25	I heard		
6	I did not testify			26	We killed		
7	He wrote			27	He sinned		
8	They created			28	You (f) did not listen		
9	She did			29	She sat		
10	They (f) reached			30	Both of them (f) reached		
11	You (f) promised			31	I calculated		
12	You all wrote			32	She wrote		
13	Both of them (f) wrote			33	He stood		
14	You raised			34	I did not came		
15	You all (f) questioned			35	They (f) killed		
16	He commanded			36	You (f) all did not sit		
17	You all ate			37	You ordered		
18	They all wrote			38	He did not see		
19	You all (f) forgave			39	You (f) did not lie		
20	You remembered			40	They (f) sinned		

Quranic Practice

Drill #4

Underline the past tense fi'l in each ayah and state the pronoun along with a translation.

1	إِنَّ ٱلَّذِينَ كَفَرُوا۟ سَوَآءٌ عَلَيْهِمْ ءَأَنذَرْتَهُمْ أَمْ لَمْ تُنذِرْهُمْ لَا يُؤْمِنُونَ 2:6	
2	خَتَمَ ٱللَّهُ عَلَىٰ قُلُوبِهِمْ وَعَلَىٰ سَمْعِهِمْ وَعَلَىٰ أَبْصَٰرِهِمْ غِشَٰوَةٌ وَلَهُمْ عَذَابٌ عَظِيمٌ 2:7	
3	ذَهَبَ ٱللَّهُ بِنُورِهِمْ وَتَرَكَهُمْ فِى ظُلُمَٰتٍ لَّا يُبْصِرُونَ – 2:17	
4	فَوَجَدَا عَبْدًا مِّنْ عِبَادِنَا آتَيْنَٰهُ رَحْمَةً مِّنْ عِندِنَا وَعَلَّمْنَٰهُ مِن لَّدُنَّا عِلْمًا – 18:65	
5	وَيَقْطَعُونَ مَا أَمَرَ ٱللَّهُ بِهِ أَن يُوصَلَ وَيُفْسِدُونَ فِى ٱلْأَرْضِ – 2:27	
6	وَإِذْ قَالَ رَبُّكَ لِلْمَلَٰٓئِكَةِ إِنِّى جَاعِلٌ فِى ٱلْأَرْضِ خَلِيفَةً – 2:30	
7	وَإِذْ أَخَذْنَا مِيثَٰقَكُمْ وَرَفَعْنَا فَوْقَكُمُ ٱلطُّورَ – 2:63	
8	ٱدْخُلُوا۟ عَلَيْهِمُ ٱلْبَابَ فَإِذَا دَخَلْتُمُوهُ فَإِنَّكُمْ غَٰلِبُونَ – 5:23	
9	وَإِذْ قَتَلْتُمْ نَفْسًا فَٱدَّٰرَأْتُمْ فِيهَا – 2:72	
10	فَوَيْلٌ لَّهُم مِّمَّا كَتَبَتْ أَيْدِيهِمْ وَوَيْلٌ لَّهُم مِّمَّا يَكْسِبُونَ – 2:79	
11	بَلَىٰ مَن كَسَبَ سَيِّئَةً وَأَحَاطَتْ بِهِ خَطِيٓئَتُهُ – 2:81	
12	وَلَن يَتَمَنَّوْهُ أَبَدًا بِمَا قَدَّمَتْ أَيْدِيهِمْ ۚ وَٱللَّهُ عَلِيمٌ بِٱلظَّٰلِمِينَ – 2:95	
13	وَمَنْ أَظْلَمُ مِمَّن مَّنَعَ مَسَٰجِدَ ٱللَّهِ 2:114	
14	يَٰقَوْمِ إِنَّكُمْ ظَلَمْتُمْ أَنفُسَكُم بِٱتِّخَاذِكُمُ ٱلْعِجْلَ 4:147	
15	وَأَتْمَمْتُ عَلَيْكُمْ نِعْمَتِى وَرَضِيتُ لَكُمُ ٱلْإِسْلَٰمَ دِينًا 5:3	

Past Tense with Attached Pronouns

Plural	جمع	Dual	تثنية	Singular	واحد	
Them	هُمْ	Them(2)	هُمَا	Him	هُ	3rd M
Their(F)	هُنَّ	Them(2)(F)	هُمَا	Her	هَا	3rd F
You(all)	كُمْ	You(2)	كُمَا	You	كَ	2nd M
You(all)(F)	كُنَّ	You(2)(F)	كُمَا	You(F)	كِ	2nd F
Us		نَا		Me	ني	1st

Attached Pronouns with Verbs

Examples:

نَصَرَهُ	I helped him	سَمِعْنَكُمْ	They (f) heard you(all)
شَكَرْتَهُمْ	You thanked them	شَكَرْتُمَاهُمْ	Both of you (m/f) thanked them
سَأَلُوْكَ	They questioned you	قَتَلْنَهَا	They (f) killed her
ضَرَبَتْنِي	She hit me	ظَلَمَتَاكُنَّ	They(2)(F) oppressed you(all)(F)
نَصَرْتُكُمْ	I helped/aided you(all)	مَنَعَكَ	He refused you
بَصُرْتُنَّنَا	You all (f) saw us	عَلِمَهَا	He knew her

Past Tense With Attached Pronoun Practice

Drill #5

Translate the following words into English and state the pronoun within each Fi'l.

	Arabic word	English Translation	Pronoun		Arabic Word	English Translation	Pronoun
1	نَصَرَهَا			8	كَرُمَتَاكُمَا		
2	عَلِمْتُمَاهُمْ			9	سَمِعُوهُنَّ		
3	سَأَلْتُكُمْ			10	خَلَقْنَاكُمْ		
4	قَتَلَاهُمَا			11	تَرَكُهُمْ		
5	رَزَقْنَاهُمْ			12	ضَرَبْتِهَا		
6	أَمَرَكَ			13	نَصَرْتَهُنَّ		
7	جَعَلْتُكُنَّ			14	أَمَرْتُمُوهُمْ		

Translate the following sentences into Arabic

	English word	Arabic translation		English word	Arabic translation
1	You all (m) helped them		8	He helped me	
2	They made you all		9	We did not forgive him	
3	He created them (2)		10	You gave them (f)	
4	We made you (2)		11	They (f) made you all (f)	
5	She hit you all		12	They(2)(f) heard you (f)	
6	You all commanded her		13	We killed them (f)	
7	We left you all		14	You (f) hit her	

Review

Drill #6

Match the following Arabic words with their appropriate translations:

صَبَرُوْا	Both of them killed
نَذَرْنَ	She remembered
رَفَعْتُمَا	You (f) left
مَارَسْتَ	She reached
مَنَعْتُمْ	They were patient
قَتَلَا	They (f) disbelieved
ذَكَرَتْ	Both of you raised
بَلَغَتْ	They (f) warned
ذَهَبْتِ	You practiced
كَفَرْنَ	You all forbade

Translate the following English sentences into Arabic. Use this word bank along with the word bank in the beginning of the chapter to help with vocabulary.

الطَّعَامُ	The food	كِتَابٌ	A Book	الْوَلَدُ	The boy	فِيْ	in
الْبَيْتُ	The House	أَقْلَامُ	Pens	الْمَدْرَسَةُ	The school		

They both ate the food	
She wrote a book	
They all broke pens	
He reached the school	
They all left the house	
She forgave the boy	
He read the book	
You (f) all saw the book	
They all sat in the school	
We studied the book	

Vocabulary Crosswords

VIRTUOUS QUALITIES — URBAN OBJECTS

English to Arabic:

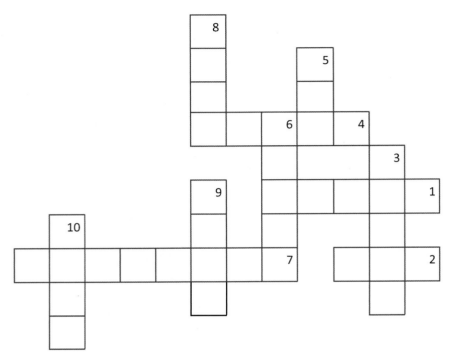

DOWN	ACROSS
3. street	1. buses
5. generosity	2. honor
6. sincerity	4. trust worthi-ness
8. strength	7. pharmacies
9. hotel	
10. righteous	

Arabic to English:

DOWN	ACROSS
2. صَيْدَلِيَةٌ	1. تَوَكُّلٌ
6. تَوَاضُعٌ	3. مَدِيْنَةٌ
7. عِلْمٌ	4. مَبَانِي
9. كَرَمٌ	5. أَرْصِفَةٌ
10. حَافِلَةٌ	8. حَارَةٌ

Present Tense Verbs

Present Tense

فِعْلٌ مُضَارِعٌ

Plural	جمع		Dual	تثنية		Singular	واحد		
They help	يَنْصُرُوْنَ	هُمْ	They(2) help	يَنْصُرَانِ	هُمَا	He helps	يَنْصُرُ	هُوَ	3rd M
They(F) help	يَنْصُرْنَ	هُنَّ	They(2)(F) help	تَنْصُرَانِ	هُمَا	She helps	تَنْصُرُ	هِيَ	3rd F
You(all) help	تَنْصُرُوْنَ	أَنْتُمْ	You(2) help	تَنْصُرَانِ	أَنْتُمَا	You help	تَنْصُرُ	أَنْتَ	2nd M
You(all)(F) help	تَنْصُرْنَ	أَنْتُنَّ	You(2)(F) help	تَنْصُرَانِ	أَنْتُمَا	You(F) help	تَنْصُرِيْنَ	أَنْتِ	2nd F
We help			نَنْصُرُ	نَحْنُ		I help	أَنْصُرُ	أَنَا	1st

Try some oral drills:

ش ر ب	س أ ل	ف ت ح	ر ف ع	أ ك ل	ف ع ل	أ خ ذ	م ل ع	ذ ه ب	ن ص ر

When you have learnt the Present Tense charts please find 3 different people in your class to sign off your charts and after that read it to the instructor/TA for final sign off

Present Tense Chart—Memorization Tracker				
Verb	Person 1	Person 2	Person 3	Instructor/TA
فِعْل مُضَارِع				

Tip: Negating in the present tense: Use the harf لَا

Present Tense Practice Charts

Drill #7

Plural جَمْعٌ		Dual مُثَنَّى		Singular مُفْرَدٌ		
	هُمْ		هُمَا		هُوَ	3rd
	هُنَّ		هُمَا		هِيَ	3rd
	أَنْتُمْ		أَنْتُمَا		أَنْتَ	2nd
	أَنْتُنَّ		أَنْتُمَا		أَنْتِ	2nd
			نَحْنُ		أَنَا	1st

Plural جَمْعٌ		Dual مُثَنَّى		Singular مُفْرَدٌ		
	هُمْ		هُمَا		هُوَ	3rd
	هُنَّ		هُمَا		هِيَ	3rd
	أَنْتُمْ		أَنْتُمَا		أَنْتَ	2nd
	أَنْتُنَّ		أَنْتُمَا		أَنْتِ	2nd
			نَحْنُ		أَنَا	1st

Plural جَمْعٌ		Dual مُثَنَّى		Singular مُفْرَدٌ		
	هُمْ		هُمَا		هُوَ	3rd
	هُنَّ		هُمَا		هِيَ	3rd
	أَنْتُمْ		أَنْتُمَا		أَنْتَ	2nd
	أَنْتُنَّ		أَنْتُمَا		أَنْتِ	2nd
			نَحْنُ		أَنَا	1st

Present Tense Translation Practice

Drill #8

Translate the following words into English and state the pronoun within each Fi'l.

	Arabic Word	English translation	Pronoun		Arabic Word	English Translation	Pronoun
1	يَفْسُقُ			19	يَذْهَبْنَ		
2	يَفْسُقَانِ			20	تَأْخُذُ		
3	تَصْبِرُوْنَ			21	لَاتَبْلُغَانِ		
4	لَايَقْرَأُ			22	يَشْكُرْنَ		
5	لَا تَخْرُجُ			23	تَغْفِرُ		
6	تَذْكُرَانِ			24	تَخْرُجَانِ		
7	لَايَفْعَلْنَ			25	يَسْمَعْنَ		
8	تَقُوْمُ			26	تَرْفَعُ		
9	تَأْمُرُوْنَ			27	تَظْلِمِيْنَ		
10	تَخْلُقُ			28	يَجْلِسُ		
11	تَكْسِبْنَ			29	لَاتَخْلُقِيْنَ		
12	يَجْعَلَانِ			30	تَفْتَحُوْنَ		
13	تَجْلِسِيْنَ			31	لَايَنْصُرُوْنَ		
14	تَكْفُرُ			32	أَذْهَبُ		
15	يَنْذُرْنَ			33	لَاأَلْعَبُ		
16	تَنْصُرْنَ			34	لَانَفْسُقُ		
17	يَكْسِبُ			35	تَسْأَلُ		
18	نَنْصُرُ			36	يَنْظُرَانِ		

Present Tense Arabic Translation Practice

Drill #9

Translate the following words into Arabic and state the pronoun each Fi'l.

	English word	Arabic translation	Pronoun		English word	Arabic translation	Pronoun
1	He creates			21	They all remember		
2	She knows			22	We raise		
3	We eat			23	She witnesses		
4	We leave			24	You stand up		
5	They (f) prevent			25	They all sit		
6	You gather			26	They (f) go		
7	Both of you hit			27	You (f) read		
8	Both of them sit			28	He reads		
9	They all command			29	Both of you take		
10	They (f) disbelieve			30	They (f) raise		
11	We warn			31	You question		
12	Both of them write			32	Both of them help		
13	We hear			33	You (f) do		
14	All of you become weak			34	All of you question		
15	We question			35	She makes		
16	All of you earn			36	You (f) kill		
17	You (f) wrong			37	I write		
18	He tries			38	They all establish		
19	You all (f) be patient			39	You all (f) help		
20	I hit			40	I command		

Quranic Practice

Drill #10

Identify the present tense fi'l in each ayah and state the pronoun along with a translation.

1	إِيَّاكَ نَعْبُدُ وَإِيَّاكَ نَسْتَعِينُ - 1:5	
2	بِمَا كَانُوا بِآيَاتِنَا يَظْلِمُونَ - 7:9	
3	قَلِيلًا مَّا تَشْكُرُونَ - 7:10	
4	أَتَقُولُونَ عَلَى اللَّهِ مَا لَا تَعْلَمُونَ - 7:28	
5	وَقَالَتْ أُولَاهُمْ لِأُخْرَاهُمْ فَمَا كَانَ لَكُمْ عَلَيْنَا مِن فَضْلٍ فَذُوقُوا الْعَذَابَ بِمَا كُنتُمْ تَكْسِبُونَ - 7:39	
6	وَنَادَىٰ أَصْحَابُ الْأَعْرَافِ رِجَالًا يَعْرِفُونَهُم بِسِيمَاهُمْ - 7:48	
7	أَهَٰؤُلَاءِ الَّذِينَ أَقْسَمْتُمْ لَا يَنَالُهُمُ اللَّهُ بِرَحْمَةٍ ادْخُلُوا الْجَنَّةَ لَا خَوْفٌ عَلَيْكُمْ وَلَا أَنتُمْ تَحْزَنُونَ - 7:49	
8	ادْعُوا رَبَّكُمْ تَضَرُّعًا وَخُفْيَةً إِنَّهُ لَا يُحِبُّ الْمُعْتَدِينَ - 7:55	
9	فَلَمَّا كَشَفْنَا عَنْهُمُ الرِّجْزَ إِلَىٰ أَجَلٍ هُم بَالِغُوهُ إِذَا هُمْ يَنكُثُونَ - 7:135	
10	قَالُوا يَامُوسَى اجْعَل لَّنَا إِلَٰهًا كَمَا لَهُمْ آلِهَةٌ قَالَ إِنَّكُمْ قَوْمٌ تَجْهَلُونَ - 7:138	
11	وَإِذْ يَمْكُرُ بِكَ الَّذِينَ كَفَرُوا لِيُثْبِتُوكَ أَوْ يَقْتُلُوكَ أَوْ يُخْرِجُوكَ وَيَمْكُرُونَ وَيَمْكُرُ اللَّهُ وَاللَّهُ خَيْرُ الْمَاكِرِينَ - 8:30	
12	إِذْ تَسْتَغِيثُونَ رَبَّكُمْ فَاسْتَجَابَ لَكُمْ أَنِّي مُمِدُّكُم بِأَلْفٍ مِّنَ الْمَلَائِكَةِ مُرْدِفِينَ - 8:9	

Present Tense Matching

Match the following Arabic words with their appropriate translations:

Arabic	Translation
تَصْبِرُوْنَ	You Practice
تَرْفَعْ	I Earn
تُمَارِسْ	You all are Patient
تَكْفُرُ	You both Remember
تُجَاهِدُوْنَ	You all Struggle
أَكْسِبُ	You Raise
تَذْكُرَانِ	You all Command
أَذْهَبُ	You Disbelieve
تَأْمُرُوْنَ	You Take
تَأْخُذُ	I Go

الطَّعَامُ	The food	كِتَابٌ	A Book	الْوَلَدُ	The boy	فِيْ	in
الْبَيْتُ	The House	أَقْلَامٌ	Pens	الْمَدْرَسَةُ	The school		

They both are eating the food	
She is writing a book	
They all are breaking the pens	
He is reaching the school	
They all are leaving the house	
You(f) are forgiving the boy	
I am reading the book	
They are both seeing the book	
They are all sitting in the school	
You are studying the book	

Vocabulary Crosswords

NEGATIVE QUALITIES — COLORS

English to Arabic:

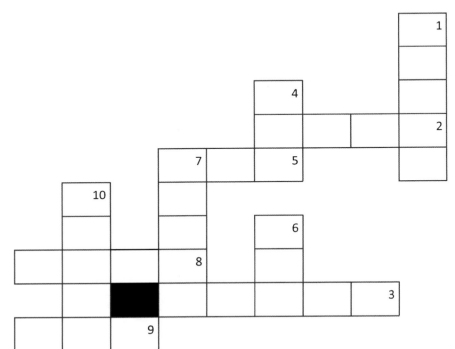

DOWN	ACROSS
1. blue (f)	2. yellow
4. association (with Allah)	3. green (f)
6. pride	5. lying
7. white (f)	8. black
10. colors	9. breaking an oath

Arabic to English:

DOWN	ACROSS
4. رِيَاءٌ	1. جُبْنٌ
6. صَفْرَاءُ	2. غَضَبٌ
9. أَزْرَقُ	3. لَوْنٌ
10. ظُلْمٌ	5. حَمْرَاءُ
	7. كِبْرٌ
	8. بُنِّي

Variations of
Verb Patterns

Impact Words

When certain words come before the present tense, they can impact the present tense in terms of the meaning and the spelling of the present tense. They affect the ending of the word. These impact words are called Harf/Huroof in Arabic. Harf can be referred as "particles" in English. There are 2 kinds of "impact words" that can alter the present tense. They are called Huroof Naasiba and Huroof Jaazima.

Huroof Naasiba

أَنْ	كَيْ	
لَنْ	إِذَنْ	

Huroof Jaazima

لَمَّا	لَمْ	إِنْ
	لَا	لِ

Naasiba	PRESENT مُضَارِع	Pro-noun	Jaazima	PRESENT مُضَارِع	Pro-noun
لَنْ يَفْعَلَ	يَفْعَلُ	هُوَ	لَمْ يَفْعَلْ	يَفْعَلُ	هُوَ
لَنْ يَفْعَلاَ	يَفْعَلَانِ	هُمَا	لَمْ يَفْعَلاَ	يَفْعَلَانِ	هُمَا
لَنْ يَفْعَلُوا	يَفْعَلُوْنَ	هُمْ	لَمْ يَفْعَلُوا	يَفْعَلُوْنَ	هُمْ
لَنْ تَفْعَلَ	تَفْعَلُ	هِيَ	لَمْ تَفْعَلْ	تَفْعَلُ	هِيَ
لَنْ تَفْعَلاَ	تَفْعَلَانِ	هُمَا	لَمْ تَفْعَلاَ	تَفْعَلَانِ	هُمَا
لَنْ يَفْعَلْنَ	يَفْعَلْنَ	هُنَّ	لَمْ يَفْعَلْنَ	يَفْعَلْنَ	هُنَّ
لَنْ تَفْعَلَ	تَفْعَلُ	أَنْتَ	لَمْ تَفْعَلْ	تَفْعَلُ	أَنْتَ
لَنْ تَفْعَلاَ	تَفْعَلَانِ	أَنْتُمَا	لَمْ تَفْعَلاَ	تَفْعَلَانِ	أَنْتُمَا
لَنْ تَفْعَلُوْ	تَفْعَلُوْنَ	أَنْتُمْ	لَمْ تَفْعَلُوا	تَفْعَلُوْنَ	أَنْتُمْ
لَنْ تَفْعَلِي	تَفْعَلِيْنَ	أَنْتِ	لَمْ تَفْعَلِي	تَفْعَلِيْنَ	أَنْتِ
لَنْ تَفْعَلاَ	تَفْعَلَانِ	أَنْتُمَا	لَمْ تَفْعَلاَ	تَفْعَلَانِ	أَنْتُمَا
لَنْ تَفْعَلْنَ	تَفْعَلْنَ	أَنْتُنَّ	لَمْ تَفْعَلْنَ	تَفْعَلْنَ	أَنْتُنَّ
لَنْ أَفْعَلَ	أَفْعَلُ	أنا	لَمْ أَفْعَلْ	أَفْعَلُ	أنا
لَنْ نَفْعَلَ	نَفْعَلُ	نَحْنُ	لَمْ نَفْعَلْ	نَفْعَلُ	نَحْنُ

Variations in Verbs

Drill #12

True and false: If a statement is false, please state the true answer.

Statement	True/False	Correct Statement, if false
Huroof Naasiba and huroof jaazima come before isms.		
Huroof Naasiba and huroof jaazima can come before fi'l madi and mudari'		
Both of these huroof have no impact on the words coming after.		
Huroof Jazzima causes a jazm/sukoon at the end of the fi'l it comes before.		

Naasiba Practice

Drill #13

Fill in the Nasiba version of the given present tense and also state the pronoun within each fi'l.

	Arabic word	Naasiba version	Pronoun		Arabic Word	Naasiba version	Pronoun
1	يَفْسُقُ			21	يَذْهَبْنَ		
2	يَفْسُقَانِ			22	تَأْخُذُ		
3	تَصْبِرُوْنَ			23	تَبْلُغَانِ		
4	يَقْرَأُ			24	يَشْكُرْنَ		
5	تَخْرُجُ			25	تَغْفِرُ		
6	تَذْكُرَانِ			26	تَخْرُجَانِ		
7	يَفْعَلْنَ			27	يَسْمَعْنَ		
8	تَقُوْمُ			28	تَرْفَعُ		
9	تَأْمُرُوْنَ			29	تَظْلِمِيْنَ		
10	تَخْلُقُ			30	يَجْلِسُ		
11	تَكْسِبْنَ			31	تَخْلُقِيْنَ		
12	يَجْعَلَانِ			32	تَفْتَحُوْنَ		
13	تَجْلِسِيْنَ			33	يَتْبَعُوْنَ		
14	تَكْفُرُ			34	أَذْهَبُ		
15	يَنْذُرْنَ			35	أَلْعَبُ		
16	تَنْصُرْنَ			36	نَفْسُقُ		
17	يَكْسِبُ			37	تَسْأَلُ		
18	نَنْصُرُ			38	تَنْسَيَانِ		
19	تَبْلُغْنَ			39	يَذْكُرَانِ		
20	تَشْرَبَانِ			40	أَكْسِبُ		

Jaazima Practice

Drill #14

Fill in the Jaazima version of the given present tense and also state the pronoun within each fi'l.

	Arabic word	Jaazima version	Pronoun		Arabic Word	Jaazima version	Pronoun
1	نَكُوْنُ			19	يَجْزِي		
2	يُؤْمِنُ			20	تَبْلُغَانِ		
3	يَجِيْئُ			21	يَشْكُرْنَ		
4	يَعْمَلَانِ			22	تَغْفِرُ		
5	يَأْتِي			23	تَخْرُجَانِ		
6	تَرَى			24	يَسْمَعْنَ		
7	يَشَاءُ			25	تَرْفَعُ		
8	يَكْذِبُ			26	يَغْفِرُ		
9	يَدْعُوْا			27	تَنْصُرِيْنَ		
10	يَنْظُرُ			28	تَضْرِبُ		
11	يَهْدِي			29	يَظْهَرُ		
12	يَرْفَعُ			30	يَرْمِي		
13	تَسْلَمُ			31	يَتْلُو		
14	يَشْرَبُ			32	يَرْزُقُ		
15	يَعْبُدُ			33	يَقْضِي		
16	يَجِدُ			34	يَجْرِى		
17	يَأْكُلُ			35	يَمُسُّ		
18	يَنْظُرُ			36	يَعْرِفْنَ		

Review Chart

Here are all of the conjugations we have learned up until now:

STATE OF JAZM جَزْم	STATE OF NASB نَصْب	PRESENT NEGATION نَفْي	PAST NEGATION نَفْي	PRESENT مُضَارِع	PAST مَاضِي	PRONOUN ضمير
لَمْ يَفْعَلْ	لَنْ يَفْعَلَ	لا يَفْعَلُ	ما فَعَلَ	يَفْعَلُ	فَعَلَ	هُوَ
لَمْ يَفْعَلاَ	لَنْ يَفْعَلاَ	لا يَفْعَلاَنِ	ما فَعَلا	يَفْعَلاَنِ	فَعَلا	هُمَا
لَمْ يَفْعَلُوْا	لَنْ يَفْعَلُوْا	لا يَفْعَلُوْنَ	ما فَعَلُوْا	يَفْعَلُوْنَ	فَعَلُوْا	هُمْ
لَمْ تَفْعَلْ	لَنْ تَفْعَلَ	لا تَفْعَلُ	ما فَعَلَتْ	تَفْعَلُ	فَعَلَتْ	هِيَ
لَمْ تَفْعَلاَ	لَنْ تَفْعَلاَ	لا تَفْعَلاَنِ	ما فَعَلَتَا	تَفْعَلاَنِ	فَعَلَتَا	هُمَا
لَمْ يَفْعَلْنَ	لَنْ يَفْعَلْنَ	لا يَفْعَلْنَ	ما فَعَلْنَ	يَفْعَلْنَ	فَعَلْنَ	هُنَّ
لَمْ تَفْعَلْ	لَنْ تَفْعَلَ	لا تَفْعَلُ	ما فَعَلْتَ	تَفْعَلُ	فَعَلْتَ	أَنْتَ
لَمْ تَفْعَلاَ	لَنْ تَفْعَلاَ	لا تَفْعَلاَنِ	ما فَعَلْتُمَا	تَفْعَلاَنِ	فَعَلْتُمَا	أَنْتُمَا
لَمْ تَفْعَلُوْا	لَنْ تَفْعَلُوْا	لا تَفْعَلُوْنَ	ما فَعَلْتُمْ	تَفْعَلُوْنَ	فَعَلْتُمْ	أَنْتُمْ
لَمْ تَفْعَلِيْ	لَنْ تَفْعَلِيْ	لا تَفْعَلِيْنَ	ما فَعَلْتِ	تَفْعَلِيْنَ	فَعَلْتِ	أَنْتِ
لَمْ تَفْعَلاَ	لَنْ تَفْعَلاَ	لا تَفْعَلاَنِ	ما فَعَلْتُمَا	تَفْعَلاَنِ	فَعَلْتُمَا	أَنْتُمَا
لَمْ تَفْعَلْنَ	لَنْ تَفْعَلْنَ	لا تَفْعَلْنَ	ما فَعَلْتُنَّ	تَفْعَلْنَ	فَعَلْتُنَّ	أَنْتُنَّ
لَمْ أَفْعَلْ	لَنْ أَفْعَلَ	لا أَفْعَلُ	ما فَعَلْتُ	أَفْعَلُ	فَعَلْتُ	أنا
لَمْ نَفْعَلْ	لَنْ نَفْعَلَ	لا نَفْعَلُ	ما فَعَلْنَا	نَفْعَلُ	فَعَلْنَا	نَحْنُ

Command Verbs

Command Verbs

فَعل أمر

Conjugations for 2nd Person حاضِر are created by THREE/FOUR steps:

1. Conjugate the verb to present tense verb to a state of jazm (جَزْم)

2. Drop the ت prefix of the present tense verb

3. After dropping ت prefix if the left over word do not start with a sukoon then that is the final command verb. If it starts with a sukoon then add an Alif

4. If the ع Kalima has a Dhumma then put a dhumma on the Alif otherwise give a Kasrah to the Alif

Step # 4 Put Harakah on Alif	Harakah on ع Kalimah	Step # 3 Do we need Alif?	Step # 2 Drop Prefix ت	Step # 1 STATE OF JAZM	2nd Person PRESENT مُضارع
اُنْصُرْ	Dhumma	انْصُرْ	نْصُرْ	تَنْصُرْ	تَنْصُرُ
اِفْتَحْ	Fatha	افْتَحْ	فْتَحْ	تَفْتَحْ	تَفْتَحُ
اِضْرِبْ	Kasrah	اضْرِبْ	ضْرِبْ	تَضْرِبْ	تَضْرِبُ
		جَاهِدْ	جَاهِدْ	تُجَاهِدْ	تُجَاهِدُ
اُنْصُرُوْا	Dhumma	انْصُرُوْا	نْصُرُوْا	تَنْصُرُوْا	تَنْصُرُوْنَ
اِفْتَحِيْ	Fatha	افْتَحِيْ	فْتَحِيْ	تَفْتَحِيْ	تَفْتَحِيْنَ
اِضْرِبْنَ	Kasrah	اضْرِبْنَ	ضْرِبْنَ	تَضْرِبْنَ	تَضْرِبْنَ
اِجْعَلَا	Fatha	اجْعَلَا	جْعَلَا	تَجْعَلَا	تَجْعَلَانِ

Commanding Conversion Practice

Drill #15

construct commanding fi'l from the given root letters and pronouns.

Step # 4 Put Harakah on Alif	Harakah on ع Kalimah	Step # 3 Do we need Alif?	Step # 2 Drop Prefix ت	Step # 1 STATE OF JAZM	PRESENT مُضارِع	Root Letter	Pro-noun
						ف س ق	أَنْتُمْ
						ظ ل م	أَنْتَ
						ر ف ع	أَنْتُمَا
						خ ل ق	أَنْتُنَّ
						س أ ل	أَنْتِ
						س م ع	أَنْتُمْ
						ر ك ب	أَنْتَ
						غ ف ر	أَنْتُمَا
						ض ر ب	أَنْتُنَّ
						ن ذ ر	أَنْتُمَا
						ب ل غ	أَنْتِ
						ص ب ر	أَنْتُنَّ
						ذ ك ر	أَنْتَ
						ك س ر	أَنْتُمْ

Commanding Translation Practice

Drill #16

Translate the given commands and the pronoun within

	Commanding Fi'l	English translation	Pronoun		Commanding Fi'l	English translation	Pronoun
1	اُنْصُرْ			11	اُشْكُرْ		
2	اِذْهَبِي			12	اِجْلَسِي		
3	قُوْلَا			13	اُذْكُرْ		
4	اِعْمَلْنَ			14	قُلْنَ		
5	اِسْمَعْ			15	اِرْكَبْنَ		
6	اِرْجِعُوْا			16	اُدْرُسْ		
7	اِشْرَبْ			17	اِذْهَبَا		
8	اِرْفَعَا			18	اِرْفَعْ		
9	اُقْتُلُوْا			19	اِشْهَدَا		
10	اِمْنَعْ			20	اُرْزُقُوْا		

Commanding Practice

Drill #17

Write the Amr (Command)

الامر	مضارع	ماضى	Meaning	الامر	مضارع	ماضى	Meaning
	يَحْبِسُ	حَبَسَ	to imprison		يَبْذُلُ	بَذَلَ	to spend
	يَبْسُطُ	بَسَطَ	to spread		يَجْذِبُ	جَذَبَ	to pull
	يَخْدَعُ	خَدَعَ	to cheat		يَرْغَبُ	رَغِبَ	to desire
	يَشْهَدُ	شَهِدَ	to witness		يَحْرُثُ	حَرَثَ	to cultivate
	يَحْشُرُ	حَشَرَ	to gather		يَخْبُثُ	خَبُثَ	to be bad
	يَحْذِفُ	حَذَفَ	to omit		يَنْعِمُ	نَعِمَ	to live in luxury
	يَضْحَكُ	ضَحِكَ	to laugh		يَحْصُدُ	حَصَدَ	to harvest
	يَخْلُدُ	خَلَدَ	to last for-ever		يَدْفَعُ	دَفَعَ	to push
	يَغْلُظُ	غَلُظَ	to be thick		يَحْلِفُ	حَلَفَ	to swear
	يَسْبَحُ	سَبَحَ	to swim		يَدْخُلُ	دَخَلَ	to enter
	يَرْبُطُ	رَبَطَ	to bind		يَكْمُلُ	كَمُلَ	to be com-plete
	يَحْلِقُ	حَلَقَ	to shave off		يَلْعَقُ	لَعِقَ	to lick
	يَعْطَشُ	عَطِشَ	to be thirsty		يَرْقُدُ	رَقَدَ	to sleep
	يَرْكُضُ	رَكَضَ	to run		يَحْمِلُ	حَمَلَ	to carry

Review Practice

Drill #18

Identify whether the word is Past or Present. Convert to the other and put commands for all 2nd Form Verbs.

Form	الامر	مضارع	ماضى	Word	Form	الامر	مضارع	ماضى	Word
				ذَكَرْتِ					مَنَعْتُ
				طَعِمْنَا					تَفْتَحَانِ
				اَجْلِسُ					سَمِعْتُمْ
				كُلْ					نَضْرِبُ
				يَسَمَعُ					ضَرَبْتِ
				نَذَرْتِ					جَعَلْنَا
				ذَهَبْتَ					حَسِبْتُنَّ
				تَقُوْلُوْنَ					كَرُمْتُمَا
				تَقْتُلِيْنَ					كَرُمَتْ
				نَذَرْنَا					اِمْنَعْ
				قَرَأْتُ					رَكِبْنَ
				طَعِمْتُنَّ					ذَكَرْتُ
				تَجْلِسُوْنَ					قُلْ
				دَرَسْتُمْ					طَعِمَا

Quranic Practice

Drill #19

Verb	Quantity	Form	Quranic Verses
			وَالَّذِينَ يُؤْمِنُونَ بِمَا أُنزِلَ إِلَيْكَ وَمَا أُنزِلَ مِن قَبْلِكَ وَبِالْأَخِرَةِ هُمْ يُوقِنُونَ
			قَالَ أَنَّى يُحْيِ هَذِهِ اللَّهُ بَعْدَ مَوْتِهَا
			وَلَقَدْ أَنزَلْنَا إِلَيْكَ ءَايَتٍ بَيِّنَتٍ وَمَا يَكْفُرُ بِهَا إِلَّا لَفَسِقُونَ
			وَيُشْهِدُ اللَّهَ عَلَى مَا فِي قَلْبِهِ
			يُرِيدُ اللَّهُ بِكُمُ لِيُسْرَ وَلَا يُرِيدُ بِكُمُ لِعُسْرَ
			وَمِنَ لِنَّاسِ مَن يُعْجِبُكَ قَوْلُهُ فِي لِحَيَوْةِ لدُّنْيَا
			وَاللَّهُ لَا يُحِبُّ لَفَسَادَ
			مَّن ذَا لَّذِي يُقْرِضُ اللَّهَ قَرْضًا حَسَنَا
			اللَّهُ وَلِيُّ لَّذِينَ ءَامَنُواْ يُخْرِجُهُم مِّنَ لظُّلُمَتِ إِلَى لنُّورِ
			وَمَثَلُ لَّذِينَ يُنفِقُونَ أَمْوَلَهُمُ
			وَإِن تُبْدُواْ مَا فِي أَنفُسِكُمْ
			أَوْ تُخْفُوهُ يُحَاسِبْكُم بِهِ اللَّهُ
			رَبَّنَا إِنَّكَ مَن تُدْخِلِ لنَّارَ
			الَّذِينَ يُقِيمُونَ لصَّلَوةَ
			وَيُؤْتُونَ لزَّكَوةَ وَهُمْ رُكِعُونَ
			وَكَيْفَ أَخَافُ مَا أَشْرَكْتُم
			كَذَلِكَ نُخْرِجُ لمَوْتَى لَعَلَّكُمْ تَذَكَّرُونَ
			وَأَطِيعُواْ اللَّهَ وَرَسُولَهُ

Prohibition
Verbs

Forbidding

فعل النهي

- Prohibition (نهي) is the act of stopping something from being done or used.

- In English, to prohibit an act we use the word "don't"

EX: Don't do! Do not Cheat!

- In Arabic, we use the لا particle to indicate prohibition (نهي)

- The لا is called the *"lam of prohibition"* and it precedes the verb.

- This لا is one of the five particles (Huroof Jaazima) that cause present tense verbs to enter the state of jazm (جزم)

Examples:

		جَمْع	ضَمِيْر	تَثْنِيَة	ضَمِيْر	وَاحِد	ضَمِيْر
Don't Help! (You)	لَا تَنْصُرْ	لَا يَفْعَلُوْا	هُمْ	لَا يَفْعَلاَ	هُمَا	لَا يَفْعَلْ	هُوَ	3rd M
Don't Go! (You all)	لَا تَذْهَبُوْا	لَا يَفْعَلْنَ	هُنَّ	لَا تَفْعَلاَ	هُمَا	لَا تَفْعَلْ	هِيَ	3rd F
Don't Open! (You two m/f)	لَا تَفْتَحَا	لَا تَفْعَلُوْا	أَنْتُمْ	لَا تَفْعَلاَ	أَنْتُمَا	لَا تَفْعَلْ	أَنْتَ	2nd M
Don't Question! (You all f)	لَا تَسْئَلْنَ	لَا تَفْعَلْنَ	أَنْتُنَّ	لَا تَفْعَلاَ	أَنْتُمَا	لَا تَفْعَلِيْ	أَنْتِ	2nd F
Don't Eat! (You f)	لَا تَأْكُلِيْ	لَا نَفْعَلْ			نَحْنُ	لَا أَفْعَلْ	أَنَا	1st

Try some oral drills:

ن ز ل	س أ ل	ف ت ح	ر ف ع	أ ك ل	ن ص ر	أ خ ذ	م ل ع	ذ ه ب

Forbiding Translation

Drill #20

Translate the given forbidding fi'l and the pronoun within & construct forbidding fi'l from the given root letters.

	Forbidding Fi'l	English translation	Pronoun		Root letter	Forbidding Fi'l	Pronoun
1	لَا تَعْبُدُوْا			1	ف س ق		أَنْتُمْ
2	لَا تَبْلُغِيْ			2	ظ ل م		أَنْتَ
3	لَا تَرْفَعْ			3	ر ف ع		أَنْتُمَا
4	لَا تَخْرُجْ			4	خ ل ق		أَنْتُنَّ
5	لَا تَكْتُبِي			5	ش ر ب		أَنْتِ
6	لَا تَنْصُرَا			6	س م ع		أَنْتُمْ
7	لَا تَقُوْلَا			7	ر ك ب		أَنْتَ
8	لَا تَفْسُقِيْ			8	غ ف ر		أَنْتُمَا
9	لَا تَخْرُجَا			9	ض ر ب		أَنْتُنَّ
10	لَا تَعْمَلْنَ			10	أ ك ل		أَنْتُمَا
11	لَا تَسْأَلْ			11	ب ل غ		أَنْتِ
12	لَا تَأْكُلُوْا			12	ص ب ر		أَنْتُنَّ
13	لَا تَدْرُسْنَ			13	ذ ك ر		أَنْتَ
14	لَا تَصْبِرْ			14	ق ت ل		أَنْتُمَا
15	لَا تَمْنَعْ			15	ذ ه ب		أَنْتُمْ
16	لَا تَجْلِسْ			16	ش ك ر		أَنْتِ
17	لَا تَفْسُقْنَ			17	ك ت ب		أَنْتُنَّ
18	لَا تَصْبِرِيْ			18	خ ر ج		أَنْتُمَا

Qur'anic Practice

Drill #21

Identify the Fi'l Amr and Nahi in the following ayaat and state the pronoun

1	اذْهَبْ إِلَىٰ فِرْعَوْنَ إِنَّهُ طَغَىٰ – 20:24	
2	قَالَ رَبِّ اشْرَحْ لِي صَدْرِي – 20:25	
3	وَيَسِّرْ لِي أَمْرِي – 20:26	
4	وَاحْلُلْ عُقْدَةً مِّن لِّسَانِي – 20:27	
5	وَقَالَ رَبِّ أَوْزِعْنِي أَنْ أَشْكُرَ نِعْمَتَكَ الَّتِي أَنْعَمْتَ عَلَيَّ وَعَلَىٰ وَالِدَيَّ وَأَنْ أَعْمَلَ صَالِحًا تَرْضَاهُ وَأَدْخِلْنِي بِرَحْمَتِكَ فِي عِبَادِكَ الصَّالِحِينَ – 27:19	
6	اشْدُدْ بِهِ أَزْرِي – 20:31	
7	رَبِّ فَلَا تَجْعَلْنِي فِي الْقَوْمِ الظَّالِمِينَ – 23:94	
8	قَالَ خُذْهَا وَلَا تَخَفْ سَنُعِيدُهَا سِيرَتَهَا الْأُولَىٰ – 20:21	
9	يَا أَيُّهَا الَّذِينَ آمَنُوا لَا تَتَّخِذُوا بِطَانَةً مِّن دُونِكُمْ 3:118	
10	لَا تُحَرِّكْ بِهِ لِسَانَكَ لِتَعْجَلَ بِهِ – 75:16	
11	يَا أَيُّهَا الَّذِينَ آمَنُوا لَا تُحَرِّمُوا طَيِّبَاتِ مَا أَحَلَّ اللَّهُ لَكُمْ وَلَا تَعْتَدُوا إِنَّ اللَّهَ لَا يُحِبُّ الْمُعْتَدِينَ – 5:87	
12	قَالَ لَا تَخْتَصِمُوا لَدَيَّ وَقَدْ قَدَّمْتُ إِلَيْكُم بِالْوَعِيدِ – 50:28	
13	يَا أَيُّهَا الَّذِينَ آمَنُوا لَا تَرْفَعُوا أَصْوَاتَكُمْ فَوْقَ صَوْتِ النَّبِيِّ وَلَا تَجْهَرُوا لَهُ بِالْقَوْلِ كَجَهْرِ بَعْضِكُمْ لِبَعْضٍ أَن تَحْبَطَ أَعْمَالُكُمْ وَأَنتُمْ لَا تَشْعُرُونَ – 49:2	
14	وَإِذْ بَوَّأْنَا لِإِبْرَاهِيمَ مَكَانَ الْبَيْتِ أَن لَّا تُشْرِكْ بِي شَيْئًا وَطَهِّرْ بَيْتِيَ لِلطَّائِفِينَ وَالْقَائِمِينَ وَالرُّكَّعِ السُّجُودِ – 22:26	

Passive
Verbs

Passive Past Tense

فِعْلٌ مَاضِي لِلْمَجْهُوْل

Plural	جمع		Dual	تثنية		Singular	واحد		
They helped	نَصَرُوْا	هُمْ	They(2) helped	نَصَرَا	هُمَا	He helped	نَصَرَ	هُوَ	3rd M
They were helped	نُصِرُوْا	هُمْ	They both were helped	نُصِرَا	هُمَا	He was helped	نُصِرَ	هُوَ	3rd M
They(F) helped	نَصَرْنَ	هُنَّ	They(2)(F) helped	نَصَرَتَا	هُمَا	She helped	نَصَرَتْ	هِيَ	3rd F
They(F) were helped	نُصِرْنَ	هُنَّ	They both (F) were helped	نُصِرَتَا	هُمَا	She was helped	نُصِرَتْ	هِيَ	3rd F
You(all) helped	نَصَرْتُمْ	اَنْتُمْ	You(2) helped	نَصَرْتُمَا	اَنْتُمَا	You helped	نَصَرْتَ	اَنْتَ	2nd M
You (all) were helped	نُصِرْتُمْ	اَنْتُمْ	You both were helped	نُصِرْتُمَا	اَنْتُمَا	You were helped	نُصِرْتَ	اَنْتَ	2nd M
You(all)(F) helped	نَصَرْتُنَّ	اَنْتُنَّ	You(2)(F) helped	نَصَرْتُمَا	اَنْتُمَا	You(F) helped	نَصَرْتِ	اَنْتِ	2nd F
You(all)(F) were helped	نُصِرْتُنَّ	اَنْتُنَّ	You both (F) were helped	نُصِرْتُمَا	اَنْتُمَا	You(F) were helped	نُصِرْتِ	اَنْتِ	2nd F
We helped			نَصَرْنَا		نَحْنُ	I helped	نَصَرْتُ	اَنَا	1st
We were helped			نُصِرْنَا		نَحْنُ	I was helped	نُصِرْتُ	اَنَا	1st

Passive Past Tense

فِعْلٌ مَاضِي لِلْمَجْهُوْل

Try some oral drills:

ن ز ل	س أ ل	ف ت ح	ر ف ع	أ ك ل	ذ ك ر	أ خ ذ	ع ل م	ب ه ذ ر	ن ص ر

Examples:

نُصِرَ	He was helped	حُشِرْنَا	They were gathered
شُكِرَتْ	She was thanked	أُمِرْتَنَا	We were commanded
نُصِرَتْ	She was helped	ذُكِرْتُمَا	Both you were remembered
ضُرِبْتِ	You (f) were hit	فُتِحْنَا	We were opened
نُصِرْتُمَا	Both of you were helped	سُئِلَت	She was asked
أُخِذْتُنَّ	They (f) were seized	أُكِلَ	It was eaten

Plural جَمْعٌ		**Dual مُثَنَّى**		**Singular مُفْرَدٌ**		
	هُمْ		هُمَا		هُوَ	3rd
	هُنَّ		هُمَا		هِيَ	3rd
	أَنْتُمْ		أَنْتُمَا		أَنْتَ	2nd
	أَنْتُنَّ		أَنْتُمَا		أَنْتِ	2nd
			نَحْنُ		أَنَا	1st

Conversion Passive Past Tense Practice

Drill #22

Convert the active past tense into passive past tense:

	Arabic word	Past passive		Arabic Word	Past passive
1	سَمِعْتُمْ		18	سَأَلْتَا	
2	نَصَرَ		19	ذَهَبْتِ	
3	بَلَغَتْ		20	فَعَلْتُمْ	
4	قَتَلَا		21	ذَكَرَتْ	
5	نَذَرْنَ		22	ضَرَبْتِ	
6	أَمَرَتَا		23	مَنَعْنَ	
7	كَتَبْتُمَا		24	أَمَرْتُمْ	
8	كَسَبَا		25	رَفَعْتُمَا	
9	خَلَقُوا		26	جَعَلَا	
10	نَصَرْنَ		27	فَعَلْتُنَّ	
11	أَخَذَتْ		28	قَتَلَتَا	
12	كَفَرْنَ		29	فَعَلْتِ	
13	صَبَرُوا		30	مَنَعَا	
14	مَنَعْتُمْ		31	أَخَذْتُمَا	
15	خَرَجْتُنَّ		32	قَامُوا	
16	نَصَرْتُنَّ		33	قَرَأَتْ	
17	عَلِمَتْ		34	عَلِمَ	

Passive Past Tense

فِعْلٌ مُضَارِع لِلْمَجْهُوْل

Plural	جمع		Dual	تثنية		Singular	واحد		
They help	يَنْصُرُوْنَ	هُمْ	They(2) help	يَنْصُرَانِ	هُمَا	He helps	يَنْصُرُ	هُوَ	3rd M
They are helped	يُنْصَرُوْنَ	هُمْ	They both are helped	يُنْصَرَانِ	هُمَا	He is helped	يُنْصَرُ	هُوَ	3rd M
They(F) help	يَنْصُرْنَ	هُنَّ	They(2)(F) help	تَنْصُرَانِ	هُمَا	She helps	تَنْصُرُ	هِيَ	3rd F
They(F) are helped	يُنْصَرْنَ	هُنَّ	They both (F) are helped	تُنْصَرَانِ	هُمَا	She is helped	تُنْصَرُ	هِيَ	3rd F
You(all) help	تَنْصُرُوْنَ	أَنْتُمْ	You(2) help	تَنْصُرَانِ	أَنْتُمَا	You help	تَنْصُرُ	أَنْتَ	2nd M
You (all) are helped	تُنْصَرُوْنَ	أَنْتُمْ	You both are helped	تُنْصَرَانِ	أَنْتُمَا	You are helped	تُنْصَرُ	أَنْتَ	2nd M
You(all)(F) help	تَنْصُرْنَ	أَنْتُنَّ	You(2)(F) help	تَنْصُرَانِ	أَنْتُمَا	You(F) help	تَنْصُرِيْنَ	أَنْتِ	2nd F
You(all) (F) are helped	تُنْصَرْنَ	أَنْتُنَّ	You both (F) are helped	تُنْصَرَانِ	أَنْتُمَا	You(F) are helped	تُنْصَرِيْنَ	أَنْتِ	2nd F
We help			نَنْصُرُ	نَحْنُ		I help	أَنْصُرُ	أَنَا	1st
We are helped			نُنْصَرُ	نَحْنُ		I am helped	أُنْصَرُ	أَنَا	1st

Passive Past Tense

فِعْلٌ مُضَارِعٍ لِلْمَجْهُوْل

Try some oral drills:

ن ز ل	س أ ل	ف ت ح	ر ف ع	أ ك ل	ف ع ل	أ خ ذ	ب ع ل م	ر ذ ه	ن ص ر

Plural جَمْعٌ		Dual مُثَنَّى		Singular مُفْرَدٌ		
	هُمْ		هُمَا		هُوَ	3rd
	هُنَّ		هُمَا		هِيَ	3rd
	أَنْتُمْ		أَنْتُمَا		أَنْتَ	2nd
	أَنْتُنَّ		أَنْتُمَا		أَنْتِ	2nd
			نَحْنُ		أَنَا	1st

Plural جَمْعٌ		Dual مُثَنَّى		Singular مُفْرَدٌ		
	هُمْ		هُمَا		هُوَ	3rd
	هُنَّ		هُمَا		هِيَ	3rd
	أَنْتُمْ		أَنْتُمَا		أَنْتَ	2nd
	أَنْتُنَّ		أَنْتُمَا		أَنْتِ	2nd
			نَحْنُ		أَنَا	1st

Examples:

Conversion Passive Present Tense

Drill #23

Convert the active present tense into passive present tense:

	Arabic word	Present Passive		Arabic Word	Present Passive
1	يَفْسُقُ		19	يَذْهَبْنَ	
2	يَفْسُقَانِ		20	تَأْخُذُ	
3	تَصْبِرُوْنَ		21	تَبْلُغَانِ	
4	يَعْلَمُ		22	تَسْمَعَانِ	
5	يَقْرَأُ		23	تَسْتَغْفِرُ	
6	تَذْكُرَانِ		24	تَخْرُجَانِ	
7	يَفْعَلْنَ		25	يَسْمَعْنَ	
8	يُطْعِمُ		26	تَرْفَعُ	
9	تَأْمُرُوْنَ		27	تَظْلِمِيْنَ	
10	تَخْلُقُ		28	يَجْلِسُ	
11	تَكْسِبْنَ		29	تَخْلُقِيْنَ	
12	يَجْعَلَانِ		30	يَقْتُلُوْنَ	
13	تَجْلِسِيْنَ		31	تَفْعَلِيْنَ	
14	تَكْفُرُ		32	أَذْهَبُ	
15	يَنْذُرُوْنَ		33	تَقْعُدَانِ	
16	تَنْصُرْنَ		34	نَفْسُقُ	
17	يَكْسِبُ		35	تَسْأَلُ	
18	نَنْصُرُ		36	يَقُوْمُ	

Review

What are the steps in making a past passive fi'l:

What are the steps in making a present passive fi'l:

What does it mean when a verb is passive?

What are the benefits of using passive verbs? What linguistic benefits do they have?

Sentence Construction

Drill #25

Translate the following English sentences into Arabic. Use the word bank provided here and in the beginning of this book to help with vocabulary.

Word Bank

دَرْسٌ	lesson	رَجُلٌ	man
زُجَاجَةٌ	glass	رَسُوْلٌ	messenger

The lesson was written	
The glass was broken	
I was hit	
The man was killed	
Zaid is being helped	
She was taught	
They (f) were created	
The messenger stood	
Allah is remembered	
She was questioned	

Review

Drill #26

الامر	مجهول	مضارع	مجهول	ماضى	Meaning
		يَقْرَأُ		قَرَأَ	to read
				خَلَقَ	to create
				عَلَّمَ	Taught
				أَمَرَ	Commanded
		تَنَزَّلُ			Descend
				كَفَرُوْا	Disbelieved
				أَمَرُوْا	They commanded
		تَجْرِيْنَ			Flow
				خَشِيَ	Feared
		تُحَدِّثُ			It will report
				اَوْحٰى	Inspired
		يَصْدُرُ			will proceed
		يَعْلَمُ			He knows
			بُعْثِرَ		will be scattered

Made in the USA
Middletown, DE
02 September 2024